DEADLY

PASTOR LARRY MORRIS

with Kristi Morris

Whatever Happened to Sin?

Deadly
ISBN: 978-0-88144-431-5
Copyright © 2010 by Larry Morris

Published by
Thorncrown Publishing
9731 East 54th Street
Tulsa, OK 74146
www.thorncrownpublishing.com

CONTENTS

FOREWORD

For centuries, countless words have been both written and spoken on the subject of the seven deadly sins. Each approach leads us to see them from various angles and perspectives. *Deadly* is an attempt to challenge us to take an honest look within ourselves, and discover these sins lurking within the dark shadows of our soul. We will discover that diagnosing the disease is the first step to recovery.

In the following pages, we will not only be confronted with our sin, but also given clear steps for deliverance. When applied, we can be on the pathway to change, with the potential to revolutionize our lives and relationships.

The following chapters started as a series of sermons. God used them in an unusual way to transform lives in my local congregation. It was this work of the Spirit that ignited the idea of turning them into book form so that many others could be challenged and renewed.

It is my prayer that God will use *Deadly* to free you from the chains of these sins, and that you might discover the freedom that God's Son, Jesus, came to offer us all.

Thanks to my wife Kristi, for the countless hours spent to help me convey these truths. I know that God will bless her efforts many times over. She is an inspiration to me and a wonderful example of Christ.

Thanks to my children, Hope and Jason. They are a support and treasure in my life. They give me great joy in being a dad.

It is with deep gratitude that I thank Roger Chasteen for the opportunity to make this book a reality. It is the fulfillment of a life-long goal.

Also, I am grateful to the Broken Arrow Nazarene Church for their encouragement. Their response to these messages helped me realize that others may find them a blessing.

Most of all, I am thankful for my Savior Jesus Christ, who has set me free from the prison of sin and death and given me life to its fullest. Praise be to God!!!

INTRODUCTION

WHY DOES SIN MATTER?

Whatever happened to sin? At one time, our culture had a healthy respect for—fear of—sin and its consequences. As a society, we were concerned about relationships with God, and we were careful to uphold the standards He had set for us. We believed that, if we stepped outside the boundaries of God's ordinances, hardship in our lives would be the result.

Yet, unfortunately, sin is now simply the new *S*-word. Talking about *sin* is like saying the word *bomb* on an airplane. If someone implies that a consequence was the result of sin, that person automatically is regarded as narrow-minded, judgmental, and out-of-touch. Society has pushed sin to the wayside. Like Elvis at the end of a concert, sin has left the building.

But the truth is, sin has not left the building. Sin is on a rampage doing awful things to our society, to our families, and to us as individuals. As I read the newspaper recently, I was overwhelmed with these reports in only one day's worth of headlines: *Wife Pleads With Kidnappers for Mercy. Love-sick Boyfriend Kills Family. Real Estate Power Broker Takes Own Life as Stocks Tumble.*

Car Maliciously Set Ablaze. And the list of tragedy and violence goes on with businesses being smashed, and riots happening in California.

How did our society arrive at this precarious place? We have convinced ourselves—fooled ourselves—as a culture that our motives are more complex than simple selfishness, which is the root of sin. We arrogantly reject sin's relevance in our circumstances, insisting we are above it. Have we become a sophisticated society that has it all together? If we look around, we may see otherwise.

God set up His principles to protect mankind from sin and its consequences, just as governments set up laws to protect their citizens from consequences. Some of these laws may feel constraining: a speed limit, a tax, or copyright law. Most people do their best to follow these laws, but occasionally people make excuses and view their actions, not as breaking the law, but as *bending it.* For example, when a person breaks the speed limit by racing down the road, he or she is breaking the law. Most people justify that it's not a big deal. People get caught and pay a ticket. Unfortunately, however, too many people regard God's laws with the same casualness.

But, you see, laws are created to protect something more valuable than the rules themselves. They are in place to preserve society by protecting its people. Laws protect human life. They protect a person's health, finances, credibility, and future. In short, the directives themselves are not as important as what they preserve. Let me point out that when God gave us precepts to live by in His Word, He gave us the Ten Commandments—not the Ten Options. In other words, God didn't write the commandments on stone tablets saying, "These are just a little something you can do if you feel like it and want to please me." No, there was nothing optional about the Ten Commandments. Rather, God communicated His strong stand on the law and, in essence, said, "If you break these standards, you'll cause damage to matters much more important than these laws. You'll wreck your life."

This book was originally written as a series of sermons crafted to encourage personal reflection. But, before we look more personally into our lives, let's look first at God's original intention for mankind.

When God finished creating the heavens and the earth, He said, "It is good." He created the land and the sea, and when He finished, He said, "It is good." He created the birds and the fish and the animals of the land, and He said, "It is good."

And then He created man. For the first time, we find him saying, "This is not good!" Actually, God liked what He had created in man and saw that it was *very* good. But God found the first thing that was not good in His new world was that man was alone. This is a very important principle because, from the beginning of creation, we have been intended to live in community, in relationships. When it's all said and done, what are the most important things in our lives? Our relationships!

When I reflect on my life, the entities that bring me the keenest pleasure are not being a pastor or reaching church attendance goals. Those are exciting, but they're not what bring me supreme joy. I enjoy delivering sermons, but even when a person says, "Oh, I got what you were saying!" that's not my greatest joy. That's inspiring, of course, but it's not my sincerest delight. The greatest fulfillment in my life comes from my relationships: relationships with my God, my wife, my kids, my mom, my family, my congregation, and others. These are where I find my greatest joy.

I have never met anyone who, on his or her deathbed, said, "I wish I had worked more." Actually, the vast majority of time, people wish they had spent more time with their families or worked more at enhancing their relationships. Relationship ties are valuable. In fact, God never intended for us to live in isolation; He intended us to enjoy quality interconnections. Relationships give us fulfillment, and ultimately, they deliver the most pleasure in life.

Yet, though relationships were designed by God to bring completion to human lives, often times they glean frustration. Truth be told, when you fight and argue at home, is it any fun? No. It's not fun for anyone when you're fussing or when you're stressed with your kids, co-workers, or classmates.

James 4:1 reads, *What causes fights and quarrels among you? Aren't they caused by the selfish desires that fight to control you?* (GWT).

God recognized the power of connections that comes when we live in community. Yet, bottom line, we live in a culture focused on individualism. And with that kind of mind-set, life revolves around what we want, how we want it, and when we want it. This struggle puts us at odds with those who get in the way of our wants. But this is clearly not what God wants. He never intended us to live this way, but sin divides us. Obviously, sin doesn't just affect the selfish; it affects those in close relationships as well. Our transgressions affect those we love dearly. When we choose to disobey God, it doesn't only hurt us, but it hurts them, too. Sin severs us from the relationships that bring us principal significance.

Consider, for example, a woman who cannot control her anger. The more she blows her top, the further she pushes away the people who love her. Her loved ones become afraid to be themselves, afraid to speak for fear of her response. Anger detaches her from those most precious to her.

Another illustration would be the husband who decides to have an affair with another woman. What is the result? As always, lust entices with a promise of fulfillment; but, after the thrill, the cost is extreme. He harms his most vital asset—his family, and loses the support of those who believed in him. What started as supposed intimacy ends in loneliness and loss of loved ones. Sin alienates.

What if we are always trying to keep up with the Joneses? Everyone becomes competition. We would hear ourselves saying, "I want what he has, to dress as she dresses, to own a car like he owns, to have her house, his job, and her husband." When we become envious of others, they become competition, and we end up keeping them at arm's length. Again, we separate ourselves from the relationships that are valuable.

Do you see the predicament? God intended us to be in company with others as well as Him. But sin disconnects us from those we need, and tragically, from God, our most valuable relationship of all.

The book of 2 Samuel, in the Bible, tells of David, King of Israel. One particular spring, when kings and soldiers normally went out to war, King David sent his army and stayed at home. In the evening, the king went up to the rooftop of his palace and looked out over the city. He saw a beautiful woman, named Bathsheba, taking a bath. Alone and without accountability, he decided to commit adultery with her. Soon afterward, Bathsheba became pregnant, so David plotted to kill her husband, which he arranged successfully. David's story perfectly illustrates that too much time on one's hands, with no accountability, can lead to iniquity. It is a vicious cycle. Isolation can lead to sin, and sin isolates us. David found himself outside of God's blessing and many relationships were ruined as a result.

Identifying Sin and Being Delivered From It

So if iniquity is separating us from what is precious, how do we get past it? How do we become overcomers of the challenges sin throws at us? Initially, we have to identify sin.

In 590 A.D., Pope Gregory the Great developed a list of seven deadly sins in which he believed all sin could be categorized. The list was revitalized when, in the 14th century, Dante wrote an epic poem called, *The Divine Comedy*. His story spotlighted the seven deadly sins and the punishments for them in hell. Through the centuries, though the list has been somewhat revised, it has continued to be an effective diagnostic tool for identifying the terminal, spiritual disease of sin in our lives. The list is the basis of this book and includes: anger, sloth, greed, lust, gluttony, envy, and pride. It uncovers the unseen facets of sin in our spirits or the very drives that cause the misbehavior.

Why are families being destroyed today? Sin. Why do we struggle in our personal lives? Sin. So, God in His great wisdom and insight wants us to identify the destructive choices in our lives, and then He wants to deliver us from them.

The purpose of this book is the same—to identify and deliver. It is my prayer that, in the upcoming chapters, you will devote time to pinpointing these sins in your life. After distinguishing the problems, you will then have the opportunity to search out avenues of deliverance for yourself as the Lord directs.

But know this. You do not have to live in sin; it is not God's intention. He wants to change you for the better and bring wholeness to your life. But the only way it will happen is if you're willing to let God get to the heart of the matter; down to the deepest motives, thoughts and feelings embedded in you.

I want to finish this introductory chapter by recalling Jesus' words in John 10:10, which tell us, *"The thief's purpose is to steal and kill and destroy. My purpose is to give them a rich and satisfying life."* (NLT)

In this scripture, Jesus gives insight into the spiritual realm, the forces in our lives that we don't see. Jesus tells us to be aware that there's a rogue who wants to take advantage of us. The thief is Satan, and he wants to steal all of the good things in our lives: our families, our jobs, our peace of mind, our health. Anything that is wholesome in our lives, Satan wants to snatch. When Jesus called him a thief, he used the Greek word *clept*. It is the root of the English word *kleptomaniac*, which is used to describe a person who has absolutely no control over theft. In other words, it is his character. He steals; that's who he is.

Jesus says it's Satan's character to *steal*. He wants to pilfer the good things going on in your life; he doesn't want you to have them. And what's more, he will do anything to take them away from you. What is interesting is Jesus' use of the word *thief*, or we might use the word *pickpocket*.

Don't let this illustration be too disturbing, but when I was a kid, I had a little bit of a fetish with the concept of being a pickpocket. What I found interesting about the whole notion was how someone could steal another's intact personal belongings without that person knowing it. I remember watching a documentary on TV that showed a guy going through a crowd, lifting off of others, and then revealing what he had done. He would steal someone's wallet by casually bumping him. I didn't, necessarily, have aspirations to grow up to be a pickpocket. But I did ask my friends if they would put a wallet in their pockets so I could steal it without their knowledge. What really interested me was the thought that somebody could be so slick. Just a bump and a crime was committed.

Jesus says that Satan is shrewd. He wants to pillage your life without you realizing it's happening. So can't you imagine Satan whispering in your ear, "Hey, time to be done with that family. I mean—marriage? Whew, get rid of it!"

If he came in and said that, you'd instantly respond, "No, no, no, this is a good thing in my life. I don't want to lose it."

If he told you that you need to give up health and tranquility, you'd instantly refute him. Yet, those blessings are virtually always casualties of sin. If Satan were clear on his tactics, you wouldn't fall for them. But he's crafty, and he desires to pirate your assets subtly. He wants to take a little bit at a time. He wants you to get angry, he wants you to have greed, and he wants you to experience all the transgression in the *Seven Deadly Sins* list. But he will, cunningly, entice you a bit at a time. These little bits will begin to wear away at the very relationships in your life, and ultimately, your relationship with God. One step at a time he will take away the good stuff from you. He is a thief.

Second, Jesus said that Satan wants to *kill*. In the language which Jesus spoke, this word *kill* meant to sacrifice something of value as with the sacrificial system of the Old Testament.

Israelites would offer their most valued animals and sacrifice them on an altar. Similarly, if Satan cannot steal from you, then he tricks you into sacrificing what is most precious in your life. But these sacrifices he tricks you into making are not in worship to God, but rather in disregard of the blessings the Lord has given you. How does the devil manage this? Remember, he is sly. Satan brings problems into your life to distract and discourage you. He brings challenges, bumps in the road, and sins of others to affect you.

Satan will try to convince you to say of your blessings, "This wasn't as good as I thought it was. I don't need this anymore. I don't want it anymore."

He's cunning and conniving. *Stay alert! Watch out for your great enemy, the devil. He prowls around like a roaring lion, looking for someone to devour.* (1 Peter 5:8 NLT)

In John 10:10, Jesus said that the thief's purpose is not only to steal and kill, but also to *destroy.* This word literally means "to trash." Satan wants to trash your life, or get *you* to. He has no regard for your value, and disdains God's blessings in your life.

On the other hand, Jesus Christ values you so much that He created you in His image and came to Earth to offer you forgiveness and eternal life. Look at the last part of John 10:10 that we read earlier, which says, *"My purpose is to give them a rich and satisfying life"* (NLT).

Jesus' character and motives are in stark contrast to Satan's. Christ loves you immeasurably and longs to give you abundant life. Rather than stealing, He gave you something—Himself. Rather than killing, He laid down His life. Rather than destroying, He offered you restoration to the Kingdom of God and all its riches.

Yet, before you can live this abundant, satisfying life, you have to identify the tricks the devil is using against you and accept Christ's riches for your own. You must say, "Enough is enough! I'm not going down this road, Satan. I'm not being fooled by your deception anymore. The Jesus I serve is showing me truth and giving me strength. He is delivering me! In Him I find genuine satisfaction."

Satan is not going to be happy about you reading this book. Hopefully, through the course of the next seven chapters, we will reveal his charades by identifying the weapons and tactics he's using to hold you in bondage. But first you must determine to be honest with yourself. Let the Spirit of God shed light on the issues that are out of sync in your life. It's not my goal in any way to put guilt on you. But it is my prayer that this book will be a tool of the Holy Spirit to enlighten you to Satan's schemes, and in turn, bring you health and wholeness. I encourage you to read this book with an open heart. Allow yourself to say, "Here I am, Lord, ready for a check-up. How can You change me?"

1 John 4:4 reads, "...*greater is He who is in you than he who is in the world.*" (NASB)

Christ's power is greater than Satan's lies. The devil wants you to believe there's no escape from darkness, failures, addictions or temptations. But God's Word assures that He is greater than the darkness and any habit or sin which holds you there. Christ's love is rich enough to honor the request of any sinner who has lost his or her way on the journey to heaven.

ANGER

On October 2, 2006, Charles C. Roberts IV, a Pennsylvania truck driver, arrived home around three in the morning after driving all day. He slept only a few hours, awoke and walked his children to the school bus stop, telling them, "Remember, Daddy loves you." He returned home, and wrote a letter to his wife in reference to their baby daughter, who had died shortly after a premature birth, nine years earlier.

He expressed, "I am filled with so much hate. Hate toward myself, hate toward God, and unimaginable emptiness. It seems that every time we do something fun, I think about how Elise isn't here to share it with us, and I go right back to my anger."

He left that note along with others for his children on the kitchen table. From there he went to a nearby Amish community in Nickel Mines, Pennsylvania. Roberts, armed, walked into the country schoolhouse and took hostages. As police arrived on the scene, he shot ten little girls, leaving five wounded and five dead. Then he shot himself.

Anger can be deadly. Not only did Roberts' anger affect those he killed and their families, but his family, too, will forever be changed by his anger. An atrocity such as this won't be the end result *every* time one gets angry. But every savagery like this did begin with anger. Jesus understood this progression and addressed it seriously.

Look at the scripture in Matthew 5:21-22, where Jesus spoke, *"You have heard that it was said to the people long ago, 'Do not murder, and anyone who murders will be subject to judgment.' But I tell you that anyone who is angry with his brother will be subject to judgment. Again, anyone who says to his brother, 'Raca,' is answerable to the Sanhedrin. But anyone who says, 'You fool!' will be in danger of the fire of hell."* (NIV)

In this passage, Jesus gave insight into the progressive nature of anger. First, he said if you commit murder, you will face judgment. A murderer deserves punishment, not only from the justice system, but also from God. But then Jesus added, "I tell you that if you're angry with someone, you will face the same judgment as the murderer."

I've read that scripture many times, and sometimes I take a step back and say, "Wait a minute, Jesus. Are you putting murder and simply being angry with someone in the same category?" Basically, He's teaching that the root cause of murder is *anger*.

Look at any murderer throughout history. It could be Charles Roberts mentioned earlier or Adolf Hitler, who resented and killed millions of the Jews. Maybe a person in a bar became irate with another and took things too far. Whatever the situation, murder is provoked by animosity.

Jesus acknowledged that anger begins as an emotion. Everyone gets angry from time to time. He implied that the danger of unaddressed anger is that it evolves into a deeper entanglement than merely a feeling. It becomes an attitude.

"Again, anyone who says to his brother, "Raca," is answerable...." In Jesus' culture, saying *Raca* to someone was, to put it mildly, putting them down. It was an expression of contempt and disrespect. It was like cursing your neighbor with a clenched jaw and criticizing his character.

When a name has been thrown in, suddenly anger has gone from an emotion to a bad attitude.

He continued, *Anyone who says, "You fool!" will be in danger of the fire of hell.* When Jesus uttered the phrase *"you fool,"* he was referring to a word used to suggest a person is godless and deserves eternal punishment. So an infuriated person who chooses this approach has progressed from a bad attitude of criticism to judging and malice. In other words, "You make me so angry; let me determine your fate! I hope your crops don't grow. I hope all your cattle die. I hope your kids get sick. I hope your mother-in-law comes and stays a month. I hope you burn in damnation. This is what I want for you, a curse upon your life!"

Do you see the danger in the progression of anger? What began as a harmless emotion becomes a bitter threat. Unattended anger went from an unpleasant feeling to a bad attitude with slander and criticism, and finally, to the desire to see pain inflicted upon the recipient. What is next but the act of vengeance itself? The most harmful vengeance, of course, is murder. Of course Jesus' whole point is to handle the emotion before it has consumed you.

Notice, Jesus said if this is not controlled, then the angered person will be *in danger of the fire of hell*. The term Jesus used to describe *hell*, in the Greek, *gehenna*, was an actual place outside of Jerusalem that archaically had been used as a place of human sacrifice. At the time Jesus walked the land, it was a cesspool of sewage and trash outside of town, where filth and refuse were burned. In that light, Jesus acknowledged: once your anger has come to the point where it's not only an attitude, but now also a curse, you are good for nothing but the trash dump. Anger has taken charge of your life, and you are no longer in control. Therefore, you are rendered useless.

Anger left unchecked can be deadly.

Another example is a little boy who had a hot temper and was always flying off the handle at his parents and teachers. One day his father thought it was time for his son to get control over his temper. So the father walked into the son's bedroom carrying a handful of nails and a hammer.

"Son," he said, "you have to do something with that temper. From now on, every time you get mad, go out to the wooden gate in the backyard. Take a nail and hammer it into the gate until you calm down."

The son followed his father's instructions. Some days, he hammered three nails; other days, ten. But every time he got mad, he was out there hammering.

The boy did that for a while, and then a few days went by with no nails. The boy came to his father and said, "Dad, I've gone a whole week now, and I haven't gotten angry. I haven't nailed any nails into the board." The father replied, "Son, I am proud of you. Now here's what I want you to do. Every day that you remain calm, take that hammer, and pull one nail out."

The boy obeyed. Every day he kept his cool, he pulled out a nail. After a few weeks, all of the nails were removed from the board. He said, "Dad, I think I've overcome my anger. I haven't thrown a fit, and I can't even remember the last time I have gotten upset."

His dad patted him on the back and said, "Son, I'm proud of you. Let's go out to the gate." Together, they headed to the gate, and the father said, "Son, it's good to see all the nails out, but I want you to notice something. Where there was a nail, there is now a hole. You may have gotten over your anger, but you still left holes in people's lives because of it."

This father's wisdom is a valuable reminder to us that we can't take back our actions. Anger damages and hurts those closest to us. It pushes them away, isolating us. Loved ones may withdraw because holes are left in their hearts. These holes came from hurtful words spoken and things done in the passion of an angry moment.

What did Paul the apostle have to say about anger? In Ephesians 4:26–27, he said, *"In your anger do not sin: do not let the sun go down while you are still angry, and do not give the devil a foothold"* (NIV).

First Paul said, *"In your anger do not sin...."*

Anger is an emotion with which we all deal. It's a natural reaction to circumstances in our lives, placed in us as a form of protection. The initial feeling of anger is not a sin. However, the sin often occurs when the angry person responds in a way that is ungodly. Even God Himself was angry at times in scripture, and we know He is all good. But His anger was always provoked by unfaithfulness and His desire to preserve what is wholesome. In spite of the failures of His people, God always looked for a way to bring them back into a right relationship with Himself. Psalm 30:5 reads, *"For His anger lasts only a moment, but His favor lasts a lifetime!"* (NLT)

So we see that anger itself is not a sin, but we're instructed not to allow it to become sinful. Scripture warns that anger may quickly cross the line from feeling to attitude if not tended to promptly.

How promptly must we let go of anger? How prompt are we talking? What did Paul write?

He said, *"Do not let the sun go down while you are still angry...."*

In other words, Paul is saying, do not go to bed angry. Why is it important not to let the sun go down on your anger? Because you don't want to let anger become your companion. When you take it to bed with you at night, it becomes just that. Like the flu, anger spreads and begins to consume you.

Paul taught believers to refrain from anger's companionship because otherwise it will *"give the devil a foothold"* in your life.

What Paul meant was that if your anger is not dealt with quickly, Satan will find a doorway into your circumstances. As the vandal who wants to trash your home and steal your belongings, he has found an unlocked entry in order to wreak havoc. Remember his goals: to steal, to kill and to destroy. Anger left unchecked gives the devil that entry point into your life.

Now, let's look a little deeper. What causes anger? Why do you get angry? Why do I?

James 4:1–2 gives insight as to what causes anger: "*What causes fights and quarrels among you? Don't they come from your desires that battle within you? You want something but don't get it. You kill and covet, but you cannot have what you want. You quarrel and fight. You do not have, because you do not ask God*" (NIV).

According to James, we get angry and quarrelsome because we don't get what we want or expect.

Many times, anger in our lives stems from a loss. It may be the loss of expectations, the loss of innocence, the loss of a relationship, the loss of a job, the loss of a reputation, the loss of a tradition, or anything in our lives that we can't seem to get back. Whatever the loss, it *can* lead to resentment in us if we allow it.

Let me offer you a couple of biblical examples of unhealthy anger due to a loss. In the Old Testament, Joseph had the favored affection of his father, but his brothers hated him for it. They took Joseph and threw him in a pit, and then sold him into slavery. All this stemmed from their feelings of having lost their father's love. In the New Testament, why were the Pharisees so irritated with Jesus? Why did they plot to exterminate Him? From the start of Jesus' public ministry, the Pharisees wanted Him gone because they were starting to lose their power.

Loss can lead to animosity. I want something, and I can't get it *or* I can't get it back. Therefore, someone is to blame for my loss, and I intend to hold that person accountable.

Identify

In the introduction of this book, I stated that we will set out to accomplish two things. First, we will identify our sins, and second, we will look for deliverance. Let's begin identifying anger in our own lives.

Anger comes in two forms: *outbursts* and *repression*.

If a person has an anger issue, it may be manifested through outbursts of wrath. Outbursts are characterized by raising one's voice, hollering to get one's way, being abrasive and quarrelsome, intimidating and insulting others, and being ready to blow at any moment. This type of infuriation is easily recognizable.

The second type of anger is a little more subtle and difficult to identify. It's an natural outflow or byproduct of repression, which causes inner havoc for the angry person. Internal destruction occurs when the rancor in one's life is like a pressure cooker. Emotions boil on the inside even though they don't always come out immediately. Nonetheless, a person seethes inside until he or she explodes or his or her health and relationships are ruined.

Handling anger with repression is generally a refusal to acknowledge the emotion. Whether cognitive or not, it's a decision to push down emotions rather than address the source of the problem. Repression is most often characterized by stubborn silence, high blood pressure, bitter sarcasm, and an overall negative outlook.

Along this line, belligerence is often a form of manipulation. I've had church members refuse to talk to me for over a month because they were mad at me. This is an example of using anger as a weapon. You may have heard it called passive-aggressive. One gets mad, crosses his or her arms and says, "I'm not going to talk to you until you give me what I want. I'm ticked-off, and you're going to know it."

Other times, individuals may hold their displeasure inside and allow the fuming to destroy them. It tears away at their insides, it tears away at their joy and peace, and it distorts their identity. Actually, they no longer see life as it really is, but through the distortion of hurt and anger. The source may not be clearly identifiable, but the internal consequences are there nonetheless.

Malachy McCourt said, "Resentment is like taking poison and waiting for the other person to die."

The Anger Workbook written by Dr. Les Carter and Dr. Frank Minirth encourages readers to ask themselves the following questions to clarify if they have an anger issue:

❏ I become impatient easily when things do not go according to my plans.

❏ I tend to have critical thoughts toward others who don't agree with my opinions.

❏ When I'm displeased with someone, I may shut down any communication with them or withdraw entirely.

❏ I get annoyed easily when friends and family don't appear sensitive to my needs.

❏ I feel frustrated when I see someone else having an easier time than me.

❏ Whenever I am responsible for planning an important event, I am preoccupied by how I must manage it.

❏ When talking about a controversial topic, my voice is likely to become louder and more assertive.

❏ I can accept a person who admits to his or her mistakes, but I get irritated easily at those who refuse to admit their weaknesses.

❏ I do not easily forget when someone does me wrong.

❏ When someone confronts me with a misinformed opinion, I'm thinking of my come back even while the person is speaking.

❏ I find myself becoming aggressive even when playing a game for fun.

❏ I struggle emotionally with the things in my life that aren't fair.

❏ Although I realize it may not be right, I sometimes blame others for my problems.

❑ More often than not, I use sarcasm as a way of expressing humor.

❑ I may not act kindly toward others on the outside, or I may act kindly but yet feel bitter and frustrated on the inside.

If you checked four or more boxes, anger is probably more present in you than you would like. If you checked nine or more boxes, you likely have experienced rage whether you are aware of it or not. And if you checked all fifteen boxes, you need to take a deep breath right now and go to your happy place for just a few minutes!

Learn to recognize anger. Perhaps answering the questions above has opened your eyes. When you started reading this chapter, you may have said to yourself, "Anger? Oh, that's not a problem for me. I could just skip this chapter." Yet recognition of anger is the first step toward healing. You will never change unless you admit that you have a problem. You'll never experience the healing power of God unless you've come to the point of being totally honest with yourself and with Him. Is anger a struggle in your life?

Deliver

What can be done about anger? What might the world answer? According to Mark Twain, "When angry, count to four. When very angry, swear."

Yet much greater wisdom is found in scripture where John wrote, *"If we confess our sins, He is faithful and righteous to forgive us our sins, and to cleanse us from all unrighteousness"* (1 John 1:9 NASB).

Remember, the initial emotion of anger is not a sin, but the unhealthy handling of it becomes one. John's advice is that if you want healing in your life, you must confess your sin. You must, first of all, admit to God that anger is a problem. Healing begins when you say, "God, I recognize that I have a problem with this. I'm coming clean. I need Your help with this issue." He won't be surprised, I assure you.

James 5:16 reads, *"Therefore confess your sins to each other and pray for each other so that you may be healed. The prayer of a righteous man is powerful and effective."* (NIV)

When James penned *we must confess our sins to one another,* he revealed that a part of the healing process is sharing with a godly friend. It's vitally important to find a brother or a sister in Christ who loves you and who won't be judgmental. Avoid those who would say, "I can't believe you're behaving that way. *I* would *never* act like that." Instead, look for someone who would say, "I care about you. I will listen to you and pray with you." Sit down with that person, and honestly explain that you're struggling with anger and want to gain victory over it. You need two things: accountability and encouragement.

Life is tough, and anger is difficult to fight on our own. We can't do it by ourselves. We need God's help, and the help of those whom God gives us to draw us closer to Him and to overcome our trials. James incited us to pray together, promising that we would be healed.

One of the most freeing things that may happen in your life this very day is you telling God and another trusted individual that anger is a problem for you. When you admit it, you'll have taken one of the first steps toward healing.

Second, acknowledge that anger is a choice. It's easy to blame others when you're mad. Have you ever heard yourself exclaim, "They make me so angry!?" If you were really honest with yourself, you would say, "I am choosing to remain angry." The emotion of anger is yours in the first place, not the antagonist's. Once you experience the agitation, you have several options. You may choose either to calmly communicate with the agitator on the subject, remembering Galatians 6:1 (NASB): *"Brethren, if anyone is caught in any trespass, you who are spiritual, restore such a one in a spirit of gentleness; each one looking to yourself, so that you too will not be tempted."* Or you may choose to hang on to the injustice, making yourself more agitated. You may choose to forgive the misdeed immediately; or you may choose to harbor the offense and let it fester. Whichever way you respond, it's your choice. You have control. If you say a particular person makes you mad, in essence you're saying that *you're* giving that person control of your life.

Quick forgiveness is the key. Offenses that are forgiven immediately do not grow into bitterness. They do not become your companions and control you.

Ephesians 4:31-32 says: *"Get rid of all bitterness, rage and anger, brawling and slander, along with every form of malice. Be kind and compassionate to one another, forgiving each other, just as in Christ God forgave you"* (NIV).

And in James 1:19, it says: *"My dear brothers, take note of this: everyone should be quick to listen, slow to speak and slow to become angry"* (NIV).

You can listen better, speak less, and slow down at making angry choices. You control your own reactions. Anger is your choice. If you're angry, it's because you have chosen to be so.

Another point to remember is that we do not live in a perfect world. In all the studying I have done on the topic of anger, Romans 3:23 has helped me the most. It reads, *"For all have sinned and fall short of the glory of God"* (NKJV).

In this verse, the apostle Paul taught that everyone has sinned. Though we are acquitted through Christ Jesus, sin is rampant in our world. Not everyone chooses to live by God's grace, nor is every human decision guided by God's Spirit. Therefore, there is no perfect place, and there are no perfect humans outside of Jesus Christ Himself.

What does that have to do with anger and how does knowing that help us? Many times we believe someone should act differently. We believe things ought to be different at the job or things ought be different in the marriage. We say *ought* and *should,* and, truthfully, we may be right. Life should be different, but it's not. People ought to behave lovingly, but they don't always. We live in a sinful world, and everything is not going to be perfect.

Sometimes we let things get under our skin that we could overlook. Many irritants are merely that, irritations. The fact is, that's just life. Understanding that not everything will go just as it should, relieves stress in our lives. In fact, we must come to the point where we do not get angry over every little thing. In accomplishing this, petty frustrations no longer control our moods.

Recognize that this is not a perfect world. Everything won't turn out as we've planned. Many of our expectations will not be met. However, the sun will still come up tomorrow. So whatever the issue is, let it go. Relax.

In the book of Matthew, Jesus explained what to do when we have issues with ones who anger us: *"If your brother sins against you, go and show him his fault, just between the two of you. If he listens to you, you have won your brother over"* (Matthew 18:15 NIV).

Jesus taught His followers to *address the issue of anger.* As always, Jesus was so wise because chronic anger is usually due to unresolved resentment. If you are chronically angry, meaning you could snap at any moment and get keyed up and irritated easily, typically it's because of some unresolved issue. The wonderful truth about Jesus is that He knows you and your struggles, and He wants to help you deal with anger healthily. He wants to help you live beyond it.

Consider this. Proper communication skills are at the heart of this scripture in Matthew. So if you've got a problem with someone, go and connect with that person. Did Christ say go and scream in his or her face? No. Did He say write a nasty letter or send an e-mail? No. Did He instruct you to tell your friends so that they can tell everyone else? No! He said if you have an issue with another, go look the person in the eye and say calmly, "I need to talk to you about this.... When you did this, I felt angry."

You see, often when individuals are angry, they tend to act irresponsibly and find themselves in trouble because of their unwise reactions. That's why it's a good idea to set boundaries ahead of time. Establish behavior rules for yourself.

For example, you might plan in advance what you will say when a co-worker tells an off-color joke. Perhaps you will say something like this: "I feel that humor is belittling and disrespectful, and I'm offended by it. I would like it if you would not tell those kinds of jokes in front of me."

Or perhaps a relative shoots an abrupt e-mail to you or a friend sends a sharp-sounding text. Modern communication is astounding, and though e-mails and texts are convenient modes of corresponding, they're not good ways to handle conflicts. They leave too many questions as to what is really being said. Actually hearing a person's voice and ideally seeing his or her expressions offers better understanding of the attitudes and intentions. Also, once something is in writing, it can be reread and may come back to haunt you. A wise person once wrote: *Use only soft, kind words because one day you may have to eat them.* Make a rule in advance never to communicate negative or ungracious information via text or e-mail.

The same is true of letters. Letters can be therapeutic and useful for clearly communicating. But again, they're secondary to actually speaking to a person. If you must communicate by letter, make a point to wait at least a week before sending it. It's also a good idea to have a trusted friend read it and give you an honest evaluation of it ahead of time.

Nevertheless, the model method of conflict resolution will always be face-to-face communication. Of course at times, that's impossible so the next best thing would be to pick up the phone. At least in that method you'll benefit from a two-way conversation.

Then again, perhaps you have deeply-embedded anger from the past, and the person with whom you are angry can no longer be confronted. Yet, Jesus said if you have an issue, go and talk. In that instance, you could find a Christian brother or sister you can sit with and share what happened. Let him or her help you resolve the conflict in your life.

The truth is, if you pursue healing and resolution, you likely will find yourself much less angry and much more peaceful. You may even discover that the person you demonized was not as bad as you remembered or at least you might come to understand the other side of the situation.

Next, *let God settle it.* In Deuteronomy 32:35 the Almighty spoke, "*I will take revenge; I will pay them back*" (NLT).

In reality, too many times we want to play God. We want to do His job and fix our own problems by making sure the hurtful person gets what's coming to him or her. We're often angered when someone gets away with an offense with no obvious repercussion. We're upset because that person deserves punishment, but didn't get it. They were mean, ugly, and hateful, but didn't receive any consequences. But know this: God sees all. One day every one of us will stand before Him in judgment. He is the final and righteous judge, and we can trust Him to hand down justice where it's deserved. Leave vengeance to Him; clearly He knows best.

It helps to remember that God cares for His people and is righteously angry when they are oppressed. Often in Scripture, He defended the poor and came down on His own people for mistreating them. He instructed His people to act justly and to care for the needy and disadvantaged. It displeased Him greatly when they did not.

Romans 12:19-21 reads, *"Do not take revenge, my friends, but leave room for God's wrath, for it is written: 'It is mine to avenge; I will repay,' says the Lord. On the contrary: 'If your enemy is hungry, feed him; if he is thirsty, give him something to drink. In doing this, you will heap burning coals on his head.' Do not be overcome by evil, but overcome evil with good"* (NLT).

Scripture teaches that the best way to repay evil is by treating someone—even someone who doesn't deserve it—with kindness. When we replace evil with good, we stop the cycle of wrath.

Remember the earlier story about Charles Roberts? After the shooting in the schoolhouse, the Amish community went to the local bank and opened a trust fund for the family of the man who had killed their own children. They knew there would be funeral expenses for the now single-parent home. So they raised money for the killer's family. They offered forgiveness and stopped the cycle of animosity.

The common response is, "You did this to me, so I'm going to get you back." The more common response is all about an eye for an eye and a tooth for a tooth. Then, you get me back for getting you back; then I get you back for getting me back for getting you back. It could continue on and on and never stop. Each hurtful deed leads to another, and all the while the people involved continue to be angry and continue pursuing revenge.

Somewhere the cycle has to stop. Let it end with you by offering undeserved forgiveness. Leave revenge to the God who sees all.

You cannot do this on your own. It's extremely difficult to do good to those who hurt you. But with the Spirit of Christ dwelling in your heart and your quality decision to live in His strength, He can take your anger and bring good out of it. Yet, before that can happen, you must recognize that you have anger, and you must let Him take control of it.

Could it be that if the issues prompting your anger were completely surrendered to Him, He would use the passion of that issue to generate something productive in you rather than something damaging? Is it possible that redeemed anger—shaped by God—is the passion needed to change the world? Maybe God wants to use your circumstance to positively change the world around you.

Consider William Wilberforce, who lived in the 1700s, in Great Britain. As a member of Parliament, he gave his life to Christ and became deeply troubled by the slave trade occurring in the ports of England. He recognized that God did not want any human being treated in that manner. Through his anger and frustration at this atrocity, he overcame overwhelming adversity to abolish the slave trade.

Realize that God wants to use your anger in order to bring good from it as well.

In the movie *Forrest Gump*, Forrest had a girlfriend named Jenny. He loved her and was her best friend. She lived in a little shack in the middle of a wheat field, where, as a very young child, she was severely abused by her dad. As she grew older, Jenny internalized the anger she held toward her father, moved away and became involved in drugs, illicit sex, and relationships that destroyed her life.

One day Jenny came to her senses and came back to Forrest, knowing she could count on him. As they took a walk down a country road, they found themselves in that wheat field looking at the dilapidated shack. Her father was dead, but all the pain and memories started surfacing. Jenny began to weep. She reached down, picked up a rock and threw it at the shack, breaking a window. She picked up another and hurled it. Again, she picked up another and then another until finally she fell to the ground in despair. As she lay on the ground weeping, Forrest put his arm around her and said, "Sometimes there just aren't enough rocks."

Are you hurling rocks at everyone who gets close to you? Does your anger scream, "Get away from me! I've been hurt in the past, and I don't want to be hurt again. Get away from me!" If so, I assure you there's a caring God on whom you can depend. He waits with His arms outstretched, longing to heal you and offer you genuine peace. He wants the rock-throwing to stop. He wants you to move beyond the deadly disease of anger wrecking your life and isolating you from the ones who love you most.

SLOTH

A man went to the doctor because he had no energy to work around the house or at his workplace. After an entire day of testing, he sat down in the doctor's office for the results.

"Doc," he said, "I can take it. Be honest with me. Tell me in plain English, what's my diagnosis?"

The doctor replied, "Well, in plain English—you're just lazy."

"Okay, if you could put that in a medical term, I'll take that home and tell my wife," the man responded.

We laugh at laziness in our culture, poking fun at those who possess this "quality." At times, when a person gets ahead with very little amount of effort, the art of being lazy is even applauded as clever.

But how does laziness, apathy—or sloth, as the Bible calls it—qualify as a deadly sin? History itself speaks.

In 1964 *The New York Times* reported a story of apathy which literally awakened America. Kitty Genovese, a young woman in Queens, New York, was returning home after work at around three o'clock in the morning. As she exited her car and walked toward her apartment, a man by the name of Winston Moseley came up behind her and stabbed her. She fell to the ground screaming for help—screaming for her life!

Several lights in her apartment complex came on, and one man shouted out his window for the attacker to leave her alone. Moseley ran away, but waited for the lights to go out to return to his victim. Meanwhile, Kitty had crawled out of the parking lot to the side of her apartment building. Moseley returned and stabbed her again. As the neighbors heard her cries, the lights once more came on, but though this scared Moseley off again, no one came to her rescue. No one called the police.

She struggled to get to the door inside her apartment, but Winston Moseley came back to kill her. This time no one—not one single person—responded to her screams at all. She died. After her death, police found that 38 people had witnessed Ms. Genovese's attacks.

Why would 38 neighbors apathetically sit back and allow a young lady to die in the hallway of her apartment complex? This question resonated across the nation, spurring psychological and sociological studies. The findings were both enlightening and alarming. Later called "the bystander effect," research found that people are more likely to do nothing to help someone in need if they're in a group. The common belief is that someone else will handle it. Thirty-eight people shared this exact sentiment that night and, because of it, Kitty Genovese died senselessly. The whole concept of sloth, or apathy, is about avoiding responsibility. And that, as this story so aptly demonstrates, can be deadly.

Identify

How would one recognize sloth in his or her life? Simply put, sloth is a lack of passion. It is indifference. It's not caring—or perhaps feeling overwhelmed, but doing nothing. It is resignation from responsibility—a careless attitude, a shrug of the shoulders, a case of spiritual amnesia.

Sloth—more commonly called apathy or laziness—is a way of escaping reality.

The sluggard will fantasize that life would be better elsewhere. For example, a woman may think that if she were married to a different man, life would be easier. She imagines everything would be improved with someone else and envisions a mate with qualities her spouse does not possess. With no effort to change herself or the marriage, she complains about what she feels she's missing.

A lazy male worker may make similar excuses about his job, believing it's always more desirable at another location. Likely, he'd be heard murmuring, "If I had a change of position…" or "…a different boss…" or "…another work environment…" or "…better benefits…" "…then I could stand it here." But the real truth is that the guy is too lazy to do anything to improve his situation outside of grumbling and criticizing. Therefore, he finds his work situation less-than-satisfying, and his exasperated employer is less than pleased with his performance.

Slothfulness obsesses over petty matters. In other words, slothfulness focuses on minor issues because the important things are too hard to deal with, and the lazy one is just too comfortable to make serious changes.

Let's say an apathetic female church member may justify, "I'll go to the church down the street because the pastor there doesn't preach on sin every week. My life is fine the way it is." She may gripe, "The pastor is always trying to guilt us into new ministries. I don't want to make any changes." Or the disengaged male worshipper is disgruntled because the song leader sings hymns or choruses he doesn't know. To him, anything that shakes up his routine or spiritual comfort is an irritant.

Actually, sloth could be characterized by knowing TV characters, athletes, and celebrities better than one knows his own family members. Sloth is a love affair with the remote control. Sloth may be eating right out of the ice cream carton or drinking straight from the milk jug. But more importantly, sloth is a lack of passion for life, a disinterest in the valuable elements of existence.

Unfortunately, it goes even deeper. Idleness is not merely a loss of fervor in day-to-day living, but a loss of passion for God. *Dante's Divine Comedy* defined sloth as the "failure to love God with all one's heart, all one's mind, and all one's soul."

How might you know if you're lax in loving God with all your heart, mind, and soul? An indication of this might be that you couldn't care less about the things that God cares very much about.

What does God care about?

John 3:16 clues us in: *"For God so loved the world that He gave His only begotten Son, that whoever believes in Him should not perish but have everlasting life"* (NKJV).

God cares about people. He loves everyone, no matter the status of life. Whether Christian or non-Christian, God loves all people and doesn't want any of them to spend eternity in hell. He wants them to have a relationship with Him. And because of that, He sent His son in the flesh to pay the ransom of sin and win those who will believe back into His family.

If you're not interested in where others will spend eternity, it may be an indication that there is apathy in your walk.

God also cares about injustice. In Isaiah 1, He criticized His people for their insincere religious rituals and accused them of chasing after gifts and bribes, rather than defending the fatherless and the widow.

In verse 17, He implored them, *"Learn to do right! Seek justice, encourage the oppressed. Defend the cause of the fatherless, plead the case of the widow"* (NIV).

Again, in chapter 10, He firmly reprimanded, *"Woe to those who make unjust laws, to those who issue oppressive decrees, to deprive the poor of their rights and withhold justice from the oppressed of my people, making widows their prey and robbing the fatherless. What will you do on the day of reckoning, when disaster comes from afar? To whom will you run for help? Where will you leave your riches?"* (Isaiah 10:1-3 NIV).

God sees all, and clearly understands that this fallen world is a struggle for mankind. He's well aware of the injustice of the human plight, and He knows life is not fair. Throughout history He has impressed upon His people to relieve this breach of integrity by serving one another, especially those less fortunate.

Can you imagine the world if every Christian took an active role in regularly assisting those in need? What would poverty look like then? What would wealth look like to God's people? Certainly, money would be desired for the benefit of relieving suffering. Financial stress would be less oppressive because of the shared burden, and hunger would be hard-pressed to find victims to ravage.

How have you been used by God to relieve the needs and afflictions of others lately? Are you moved to action when the opportunity presents itself? God wants to show His love to all people, and He wants you to, as well. If you're unconcerned about the demands and injustices in our society, it could suggest a hint of indifference in your lifestyle. Do you care about the things that God cares about?

Unlike other deadly sins, such as anger and lust, sloth is not instantly flared. Instead, sloth is like concrete. It takes some time to harden. It works its way into a being, and gradually becomes more and more callous to the situations around it.

It may seem far-fetched to imply that slacking is a sin. But, honestly, how does laziness affect a relationship? It adds tension because of unfulfilled expectations and unmet needs. As a result, there's disharmony within the relationship. Remember, God originally designed us to complete one another. Yet, what is Satan's intent? He's determined to disrupt our alliances. Keep in mind, God calls it sin because it is harmful. If indifference detaches us from the ones who care about us, then it is harmful. Therefore, it is ungodly, and ungodliness isolates us from God.

Let's look closer at examples of how disregard hinders interdependence. For instance, let's consider a spouse who needs to resolve marital conflict, but doesn't want to communicate. Eventually, the frustration escalates to the point where the spouse couldn't care less about the relationship with his or her mate. When the time comes for counseling to repair the problems not dealt with in their marriage, it's to no avail because he or she is disinterested. Indolence has set in and destroyed the marriage. If partners choose to be impassive toward making changes, it's likely that divorce is on the horizon.

Let me ask a question. Have you ever worked with a loafer? Perhaps you've worked with a co-worker who spends his or her time talking instead of working, playing free cell on the computer, surfing the net, checking football scores or exchanging recipes and generally not doing his or her assigned job. If so, you know very well that this can be a detriment to the whole work force. When that person fails to perform his tasks, who has to pick up the slack? Everyone else in the office—that's who. His fellow employees and his boss both suffer the consequences, thus fostering discontent and resentment in the atmosphere.

Apathy also damages relationships between parents and children. Parents may neglect sitting and talking with their kids or participating in activities with them. Therefore, family kinship is not developed. Over time the members become indifferent toward emotionally supporting one another or building trust, which in turn causes an environment of conflict. Along the same line, when children do not take interest in school work and parents choose not to intervene, frustrated teachers lose motivation. Then educational excellence becomes an illusion rather than a reality.

The truth is, neglect and indifference affect every facet of the world around us—even culture. The quality of a populace suffers when its citizens won't assume responsibility for its well-being. People adopt the attitude that it is up to city employees to take care of a town. They may think, *I pay my tax dollars. It's up to those folks who work there. They ought to take care of the place.* If the general public decides it is up to everybody else, what happens to society?

Society as a whole begins to disintegrate as our communities deteriorate. Schools run down, public facilities crumble, landscapes grow over, trash piles up, houses fall, and everything becomes a mess. Neighbors stop helping one another, church members stop assisting the needy, crime increases, people lose faith in each other, and there becomes a general atmosphere of distrust as well as a simple lack of courtesy. When no one cares, the infrastructure of the community suffers and relationships dwindle.

For a place to flourish, its individuals must take responsibility for its well-being. If anything good happens, it's because someone has taken initiative. Look at your own community. The good happening there is because someone became concerned and made an effort.

Lately, I've noticed a trend in the attitudes of people that says, "If it doesn't affect me or is not my assigned responsibility, then I'm not getting involved." One receptionist admitted, in regard to information that would benefit the office's clientele, "If they don't ask, I don't tell." All around us in society there's a prevalent to-each-his-own mentality, which erodes the edges of community interdependence.

One of the major reasons our nation is in the financial and moral predicament it's in is simply because we are lazy. Many Americans believe it's up to the government to solve our problems and the schools to rear our children. We readily blame others for what amounts to our own lack of discipline, while in the same breath we rave over the latest luxury. The bottom line is that if we saved more, spent less, and accrued less debt as a nation and as individuals, we would not be in desperate financial crisis today. We conveniently assume it's up to someone else to assume care of our problems, and we don't accept any responsibility.

Did you know in the last presidential election, 70 million people who could vote didn't even go to the polls? What is that? It's apathy.

Similarly, when church-goers become only spiritual takers—not givers—the family of God languishes. Their obsession is to just feel good. They bask in God's forgiveness and love, then leave church and do whatever they want. They believe there's no need to consider others. They believe it's not their business to take care of everybody else, no matter who is hurting or neglected. So often they think, *After all, that's what the pastor is paid for, isn't it?* They attend church just to soak in the good vibe and feel good. But if they don't get what they want, they simply move somewhere else and likely imply they were not "fed." Though their social habitat is changed, their lack of concern for others remains. They won't talk to others about Jesus (it's too invasive and uncomfortable), and they won't get involved in the ministry of the church (it's too political and time-consuming). The more indifference, the more the church lags. Apathy keeps the church from building the Kingdom of God. Plain and simple, apathy keeps people out of heaven.

In Matthew 25:14–30, Jesus taught on the subject of laziness with a story about three servants and a master. Let's look at my quick interpretation of the story.

The master said to his servants, "Guys, I'm going away on a journey, and I want you to take care of my stuff while I'm gone." So he divided his possessions. To the first servant he gave five bags of silver. To the second, he entrusted two bags, and to the third, the master allotted one bag.

After an extended absence, the master returned. He asked the first man, who had the five bags of silver, "What did you do with what I gave you?" The servant replied, "I invested it, and now I have ten bags of silver for you. I have doubled your investment." The master praised him, saying, "Well done, good and faithful servant. I will put you in charge of many things. Now, let's celebrate. Come and share my happiness!"

To the second guy he asked the same question, "What did you do with my money?" This servant answered, "I took your two bags of silver and invested them. Now I have four bags of silver for you!" He also received a favorable response. "Good job; well done. You have been found trustworthy. I will entrust you with greater responsibility. Now, come celebrate with me," the master said.

For the servant who received only one bag of silver, we'll read Jesus' exact words:

> "Then the servant with the one bag of silver came and said, 'Master, I knew you were a harsh man, harvesting crops you didn't plant and gathering crops you didn't cultivate. I was afraid I would lose your money, so I hid it in the earth. Look, here is your money back.' But the master replied, 'You wicked and lazy servant! If you knew I harvested crops I didn't plant and gathered crops that I didn't cultivate, why didn't you deposit my money in the bank? At least I could have gotten some interest on it.' Then he ordered, 'Take the money from this servant and give it to the one with the 10

bags of silver. To those who use well what they are given, even more will be given, and they will have abundance. But from those who do nothing, even what little they have will be taken away. Now throw this useless servant into outer darkness, where there will be weeping and gnashing of teeth" (Matthew 25:24–30 NLT).

The master inquired about his money with the third servant and received a completely different response than he had with the first two. The man who'd received the one bag of silver admitted, "Boss, I know you're a risk-taker and a savvy investor. I was afraid I couldn't please you. So I did nothing with your money except keep it hidden. I went to the back yard, dug a hole, and put it in the ground."

Do you see the contradiction? The servant explained he knew what the master wanted, but he chose not to do it anyway. The whole "work" and "invest" thing was just a little too uncomfortable for him. He was more concerned about his own personal security and comfort than his master's profit. Would you want that type of employee working for you?

Let's look at the master's response. He answered, "I could have at least gotten some interest on it if you had put the silver in the bank. I would have made at least 4%, and even that is better than nothing. But you did absolutely nothing. You are a disrespectful, self-consumed, undependable employee."

Jesus' parable portrays God as the master, and the servants as God's people. In this light, how would the master's words be interpreted concerning the Almighty and His church? Basically, God would be saying, "You are useless to me. I gave you this talent..." [Or money, or blessing, etc.] "...and you did nothing with it. You didn't care about the things I wanted, and you forgot them. You were lazy."

The spiritual principle taught here is this. Those who faithfully use in God's services the resources and abilities He gives them, will be multiplied in their usefulness. But the opposite is true as well. The one who lives like, "God, I know what you want, but so what? I'm doing what I want" is the rebellious child who chooses not to use his assets for the kingdom of heaven and risks his standing in the family of God.

In the conclusion of the parable, the master instructed the others, "Take the servant who was lazy, bind him, and throw him into the darkness. There will be weeping and gnashing of teeth."

To better understand why Jesus used this example, you must understand the cultural practices of the day. You see, in Jesus' day, there were walls around a city, and the townspeople would throw their garbage over one point on the wall. Then at night the lions would come down from the hills and prowl around the dump to see what they could eat. Even more to the point, the justice system was somewhat harsh in that day. If a man was thought to have committed a crime but it could not be proven, the officials would tie him by the hands and feet, put a rope around him, and then dangle him over the wall at the rubbish heap. The officials would leave him there all night to face the lions in the darkness.

If the man had been consumed by the large cats when the authorities returned the next day, they believed surely he had committed the crime and justice had been served. If he had not been eaten, they believed he must not have been guilty. Yet, the stress of the experience was so trying on the defendant that he often would be weeping and grinding his teeth from the anguish he had faced all night waiting for the snarling lions to eat him.

Jesus' illustration is also prophetic of the day He returns and calls His people to account for their time, talents, resources, etc. Every believer will be judged for his or her work.

In 2 Corinthians 5:9-10 Paul wrote:

"Therefore also we have as our ambition...to be pleasing to Him. For we must all appear before the judgment seat of Christ that each one may be recompensed for his deeds in the body, according to what he has done, whether good or bad" (NASB).

Does this mean we will be allowed into heaven by our works and not by God's grace? No, works are not enough. Not one person except Christ Himself can be found worthy enough on His own merits to enter the presence of God. It is by God's grace that we are allowed entry to the throne room of God. As the master in the story, it is by His philanthropy we're put in His employment. But it is by *our ambition to be pleasing to Him*, as Paul put it, that we're found faithful to this grace. Does this mean we're obligated to follow all the rules? Not necessarily. More so, we're attracted to follow His commands because we're enriched by fellowship with Him. We're driven by our desire to build His kingdom because we have discovered its value.

At the end of this story, when the lazy servant is thrown where lions scavenge, Christ is warning His followers to not put themselves in a place of risk. Remember the scripture, *"He is cunning and conniving. Stay alert! Watch out for your great enemy, the devil. He prowls around like a roaring lion, looking for someone to devour"* (1 Peter 5:8 NLT). In other words, when a person becomes useless to God, he becomes useful for Satan.

Jesus followed this parable with another in which the Son of Man would separate the righteous and unrighteous as a shepherd separates sheep from goats. Let's read His story in Matthew 25:31-46:

"When the Son of Man comes in his glory, and all the angels with him, he will sit on his throne in heavenly glory. All the nations will be gathered before him, and he will separate the people one from another as a shepherd separates the sheep from the goats. He will put the sheep on his right and the goats on his left.

"Then the King will say to those on his right, 'Come you who are blessed by my Father; take your inheritance, the kingdom prepared for you since the creation of the world. For I was hungry and you gave me something to eat, I was thirsty and you gave me something to drink, I was a stranger and you invited me in, I needed clothes and you clothed me, I was

sick and you looked after me, I was in prison and you came to visit me.'

"Then the righteous will answer him, 'Lord, when did we see you hungry and feed you, or thirsty and give you something to drink? When did we see you a stranger and invite you in, or needing clothes and clothe you? When did we see you sick or in prison and go to visit you?'

"The King will reply, 'I tell you the truth, whatever you did for one of the least of these brothers of mine, you did for me.'

"Then he will say to those on his left, 'Depart from me, you who are cursed, into the eternal fire prepared for the devil and his angels. For I was hungry and you gave me nothing to eat, I was thirsty and you gave me nothing to drink, I was a stranger and you did not invite me in, I needed clothes and you did not clothe me, I was sick and in prison and you did not look after me.'

"They also will answer, 'Lord, when did we see you hungry or thirsty or a stranger or needing clothes or sick or in prison, and did not help you?'

"He will reply, 'I tell you the truth, whatever you did not do for the least of these, you did not do for me.'

"Then they will go away to eternal punishment, but the righteous to eternal life." (NIV)

Being apathetic and lazy is serious business to Jesus. I'd like to water it down and make it easier to swallow, but Jesus is saying that sloth is a sinful disease that neglects the ones He loves. It will send some to hell.

Deliver

How can a person be delivered from slothfulness?

The first and most important step is *repentance*. In Acts 17:30, Paul wrote, *"In the past God overlooked such ignorance, but now He commands all people everywhere to repent"* (NIV). In other words, once you become enlightened that sloth is an issue in your life you have one responsibility—to repent. But what exactly is repentance?

Repentance is confessing sin and turning from it. The penitent one says, "Lord, I recognize this is a problem, and I confess it to You. Now through Your power, I'm determined to change."

The perplexity of sloth is that its very nature keeps us from admitting it's a problem, simply because we don't care. It's easy for us to slough it off as unimportant. Jesus said that there is only one sin that God chooses not to forgive, and it is the sin of blasphemy of the Holy Spirit. Blasphemy of the Holy Spirit says, "God, I hear what you're saying to me, but I'm ignoring it." The sin that God chooses not to forgive is a sin you and I choose never to confess, so in essence, it's easy for us never to confess sloth.

If you're reading this today, and any of these illustrations or warnings have flagged your conscience, it's time to change. Make a cognitive choice to take action. Begin with repentance.

The next step is to *fill your mind with good things, and beware of letting your mind become idle.*

If you're a parent, you probably know what happens when children get bored on a long trip. They start to argue and complain. On family vacations for me growing up, we kids knew just how far Dad's hand could reach from the driver's seat to the back seat. There were about three inches of clearance. We would lean back as far as we could and just miss the swat. Ah, sweet memories! The lesson I learned (besides don't make Dad mad when you're within smacking distance) is that boredom leads to negativism. Negativism leads to trouble.

The same is true when slacking turns into boredom. The bored person focuses on petty, nonsensical issues. He or she becomes negative, griping about insignificant worries. Rather than dwelling on the positive and being thankful, the person may complain, "Nothing is ever right around this house. Nobody cooks as they ought to, and nobody cleans. It's just not right, and I deserve better than this." Yet, if the person counted his or her blessings, he or she would find much to be grateful for, including food, home, and family.

Or a church member might say, "This church is ugly." "I don't like the way the musicians play." "The pastor didn't say hello to me." "Nobody cares what I want." Griping and negativism blind the would-be worshipper to the privilege of fellowship within the family of God. He or she misses the beauty of corporate worship, wise counsel, and selfless ministry.

The apostle Paul wrote, *"Finally, brothers, whatever is true, whatever is noble, whatever is right, whatever is pure, whatever is lovely, whatever is admirable—if anything is excellent or praiseworthy—think about such things"* (Philippians 4:8 NIV).

How would your world look different if you applied that verse? Your situations may not *be* different, but they may *look* different. Though you can't fix every problem, if you decided to quit being negative, to quit griping and looking for all the bad stuff, and to start looking at the positive in your circumstances, it could change you. A positive outlook improves your approach toward life and may improve the way others treat you.

If you struggle with a negative outlook on life, maybe the best thing you can do today is say, "God, I have a bad attitude, and I need your help." Then fill your mind with positive thoughts and influences such as scripture, Christian music and a tally of your blessings. Stop spending your leisure time with negative influences. Start spending time with people who epitomize Philippians 4:8.

After you've repented and deliberately changed your thought life, the next step is *daily discipline.* Anything good takes work. You've heard the phrase, *"no pain, no gain."* Don't you wish there was a get-in-shape pill? Then you could say, "Look at me. One pill is all it took." But to get into shape, you've got to eat right and exercise; you've got to have discipline. It's the same with any worthwhile endeavor.

With big reward comes responsibility. Adam and Eve discovered this in the Garden of Eden. They wanted their eyes to be opened to be like God and to know what He knew. So they stepped outside the boundaries of protection God had set for them. Against His instruction, they took a bite from the fruit of the tree of knowledge of good and evil and received more than they had bargained for in every respect. Their lack of discipline and new exposure to sin made them ineligible to eat from the tree of life. Therefore, they were cast out of the Garden.

With their loss of innocence came expectations. It's as if God was saying, "You want to be a grown-up? Well, let Me show you how to take care of yourself then. Since you're so determined to be in charge of your own destiny, go ahead. Eve, you will birth children in pain. Adam, from now on you will work the ground for your food." They wanted excitement. They wanted big change. They wanted to be like God. So God let them and gave them daily routine.

If you grew up on a farm you'd know that there's routine in farming. First it's time to plow the ground; next it's time to plant the seed; then it's time to water and fertilize; then it's time to harvest. Oh and next year, do you know what will happen? You'll go through exactly the same process all over again. There is no shortcut to getting a harvest of crops.

We humans like quick fixes. "Pastor, give me a sermon series that will pump me up and change my life. Give me something that feels good."

But real change doesn't occur from hearing a good sermon. In real life if a person wants change, he or she will find it on a daily journey with Christ. Though Jesus Christ's forgiveness and holiness are instant to the one who seeks, rewarding behavioral change transpires from guidance by His spirit in the dailiness of life. It's going to happen in the daily routine. A Christian lifestyle is still made the old-fashioned way: praying, reading God's Word, observing the sabbath, showing acts of mercy and grace, and living for God's glory in ordinary circumstances.

The lazy person is often disappointed when he or she finds living like Jesus difficult. The lazy person expects getting saved to be like taking a "Jesus" pill. The person assumes that since he or she asked Jesus to forgive his or her sins, life will be a bed of roses. The person is quickly disheartened when he or she finds that the world is still a struggle. God calls for daily cultivation of character. The Lord understands the *"no pain, no gain"* law of discipline. He hasn't put that law into motion to harm his children, but to strengthen them. But the weak-willed would rather skip the regimen and go straight to the reward. Yet, because of that, he or she misses the life lessons and character-building experiences necessary to be a mature Christian.

Do you want to be like Jesus? There are no quick fixes. There are no shortcuts. Success comes through diligence. Each day is the opportunity to develop character.

If you're indifferent to the thoughts and wishes of God, don't just shrug it off! Do something.

James 1:22 says, *"But don't just listen to God's word, you must do what it says. Otherwise, you are only fooling yourselves"* (NLT).

Ask yourself a question. Are you spiritually bored? Have you lost interest in your relationship with God? According to James 1:22, knowledge without application leads to boredom.

If you read your Bible looking only to gain knowledge, you'll think you are smart because you know a lot about scriptural topics. But if you don't apply that knowledge to your life, it becomes irrelevant and trivial. The lack of luster in your spirituality will leave you dry and uninterested in your walk with the Lord.

You can attend all the Bible studies you want. You can read all the good books. You can watch the Christian programs, and you can get yourself pumped up for the next seminar conference. But if you don't do anything with that knowledge, then it has gone in one ear and out the other. Your spiritual passion will fizzle as soon as the event is history.

Most people in church don't need another sermon; they have heard it all. It's when they don't do anything with what they've heard that they weary of hearing. This boredom eventually results in depression.

Yet, one of the most fulfilling things a human being will experience is being used by God Almighty. Occasionally, He will call an individual to perform a significant feat. But more often He calls His people to glorify Him in the daily grind, even amidst the most humble of labors.

One such example is Marie, who lives a few blocks from me. She retired six years ago and decided she needed to exercise more. As she walked one day, she saw garbage scattered about. There were cans in gutters and trash on people's lawns. It frustrated her, and she felt somebody needed to clean up that mess. In her pious disgust, she felt God whisper to her, "You're the one." From that time six years ago until now, Marie has weekly walked her neighborhood with her bucket, picking up trash.

I saw her this week and said, "Thanks for cleaning up our neighborhood. I appreciate it."

"You know," she replied, "God told me to do this project, and I find a lot of joy in it."

Marie is merely obeying what God asked her. She is using her abilities and resources, and applying what she has heard from the Lord. She is an example of the truth that there's joy in even the most menial task if we know it's what God wants us to do.

Like the servants in Christ's parable out of Matthew 25, accepting Christ's grace is like being employed into His service. This grace is bestowed on His followers to be shared, not buried. As recipients of that grace, we are entrusted to spread it. Being useful in growing the kingdom of heaven is very satisfying work. God provides His people with opportunities as well as assets (i.e., abilities, riches, time, etc.) to afford this fulfillment.

God wants you to do something with your blessings and resources. It may be going down to the homeless shelter and praying with people or serving a meal; it may be getting to know your neighbor and being a support when he or she needs it; it may mean mowing the lawn or serving in the children's ministry at your local church. Perhaps it's getting involved in some kind of community action that is changing the world for the better. But God wants you somewhere doing something actively productive in the advancement of His glorious kingdom. Even the smallest act of service may be a preparation for a future significant one.

Finally, you should *hunger for something more.*

The youth in the church I pastor recently did a "30-hour famine" to raise money for starving children in Africa. The teenagers stopped all eating on a Thursday evening at 6 o'clock and fasted until 12 o'clock a.m. Saturday. The most popular person of the night was the pizza delivery man. I would have been scared for my life if I'd been the fellow facing 350 teenagers who hadn't eaten in 30 hours. Needless to say, they were more than a little hungry when he showed up!

Jesus said, *"Blessed are those who hunger and thirst for right-eousness, for they will be filled"* (Matthew 5:6 NIV). In other words, when you get to the point that you hunger for God and long to devour what He has for you, just as those teenagers hungered for pizza, then you will find change in your attitude, actions, and approach to life. Jesus' amazing promise in this nugget of truth is that if you're hungry for God, then you're going to be filled by God!

In Luke 15, we read the story of the prodigal son, a young man who ran away and wastefully used up his inheritance before his father had even died. The son's life was spent in reckless living. With his fortune consumed, he grieved, "I'm so famished that I long to eat the pigs' slop. If I worked for my father I would not go hungry." Then he resolved, "I will return to him and beg to become a servant of his estate."

As the father saw him approaching he ran to his son, put a ring on his finger, a robe on his back, and ordered a feast in his honor. The father rejoiced, "My son was dead to me, but now he has returned and is alive!" The son was awarded his full honor in the family.

Perhaps you've been spiritually checked-out in your relationship with the Lord. The detachment of sloth has you wondering what's so special about being in His family. If so, here's the simple truth. The only way to move beyond sloth and apathy is to come to the point where you can say, "God, I'm starving for You. I'm sick and tired of being where I am, and I crave more of You." If you don't *feel* that way, but you want to be there, remember Isaiah 40:30-31, that says,

> *"Though youths grow weary and tired,*
> *And vigorous young men stumble badly,*
> *Yet those who wait for the LORD*
> *Will gain new strength;*
> *They will mount up with wings like eagles,*
> *They will run and not get tired,*
> *They will walk and not become weary"* (NASB).

Like the father with the prodigal son, we serve a God who is eager that we return to Him desiring to be a part of His estate. He will honor those whose hope is in Him.

Are you hungry for more of God? Or are you satisfied with the mediocre? There are no shortcuts in this walk, and the trail is bumpy. But this could be the start of a new journey. Repent of your sloth, and dwell on the goodness of God. Daily walk in His guidance and allow Him to whet your appetite with His love. Once you've acquired a taste for Him, your vitality will be renewed.

GREED

Greed began to inject its deadly poison into my life when I was six years old. It happened when my hometown opened a TG&Y store, which became the forerunner to Wal-Mart. One attractive novelty of TG&Y was that it boasted the first automatic door I had ever seen. You know, it was the type with the rubber pad that caused the door to open automatically when you stepped on it. The great oddity was that if you stood on the inside, the person on the outside couldn't get the door to open. I made a game of standing on the inside.

Yet, the best part of TG&Y was the toy department. It was unlike anything I had ever seen. There was one type of toy particularly that grabbed my attention: Hot Wheels. I have always loved cars and still do. In a multitude of different colors like Easter eggs, TG&Y stocked all different varieties. I realize now that the day I bought my first Hot Wheels car at TG&Y was the first day greed injected itself into my veins. I wasn't satisfied with one Hot Wheels car. No. I had to have *all* the Hot Wheels cars. If I didn't get a new one each time I went, I was on the ground throwing a fit. My sisters love to tell that they have pictures to prove it.

Indulgence of this childhood addiction was just the beginning. As I grew older, greed tightened its grip.

Greed told me that if I wore a certain style of clothes, kids would like me. So, since O.J. Simpson was an athletic star in my day and wore Spot Bilt tennis shoes, I had to have Spot Bilt. I also had to wear an Izod shirt *with* the alligator on the front. Of course, it cost more with the alligator, but that was the style for me. Along with my designer clothing, it was essential that I have the largest boombox in the school. (If you grew up in the '80s, you might relate to this story.) Greed sold me the lie that if I had the right shoes, the right shirt, and the biggest boombox, I was guaranteed popularity.

When I got into college, I discovered someone who really believed in me; the Visa card. Visa would give me $5,000 to spend however I wanted, and the amazing thing was I didn't even have a job. I thought, *How cool are these guys who would give me $5,000 to spend whenever I want? My parents don't even believe in me that much.* Needless to say, I had a great time in college. Since I was a "man of means," I *needed* to have a stereo system with the largest speakers in the dorm. And since I was the self-appointed dorm-rocking master, I had to buy all the "necessary" accessories as well. Greed was sinking its talons deeper into my life.

Though I continued to grow in credit card debt, it lost its thrill when I began to have a regular income, and I was eligible for car loans. As a young pastor with a paycheck of $250.00 a week, I thought I was making big money and could afford it. Greed tightened its hold on me.

Can you relate to the enticement of stuff? In our culture we're inundated with advertisements—messages that say, "If you drive this car, you will be admired." "If you wear this cologne, you will be attractive." "If you eat at this place you will be full, fit and fashionable." "Wear these clothes. Own these possessions. Then you will be happy."

Michael Douglas's character in the movie *Wall Street* shed light on the American mind-set when he said, "Greed is good." The content of this chapter may sound somewhat counter-culture, even un-American. But there's a good reason that greed was placed in the seven-deadly list.

How exactly is greed a deadly spiritual condition? It neglects the needs of others and focuses mainly on self. Proverbs 15:27 states, *"A greedy man brings trouble to his family..."* (NIV).

One day, when my daughter was three years old and still riding in a booster seat, I was driving down a main street in Bethany, Oklahoma. My eyes scanned the car lots as they did each time I traveled this road. When I saw a 1967 Camaro convertible my heart skipped. It was mist blue with darker blue rally stripes, hideaway headlights, and sharp wheels and tires. My stomach still knots when I think of it. As a car guy, I had to stop and look. Believing I had to have it, I inquired of the salesman, "Would you take my family vehicle as a trade for your sports car?" Well, a deal came in fast order.

I went straight to my credit union to borrow money for the difference I would owe after giving them my family car. In a matter of moments that muscle car would be mine. After I was approved for the loan, I waited in the bank lobby for the loan officer to return and complete the final loan process. Suddenly, a small voice whispered inside my head, "Larry, this is a bad idea!" Then I thought of my baby daughter and my wife and was struck by the stupidity of this trade. I took my loan papers, wadded them up, and walked out. It was time for me to grow up, and that was a turning point for me.

Craving causes a person to do dumb things. It blinds a person to the cares around him or her, because he or she is only focused on one person's needs: his or her own. The greedy one is so worried about making himself or herself happy that he or she neglects obligations to others.

In the U.S., we have had our share of financial struggles. Because of our desires to have more, we have overburdened ourselves with debt and frivolously purchased things we could not afford with money we didn't have. Our self-consumed lifestyles are leaving us blind to the desperate needs in our world.

According to FAO Director-General Jacques Diouf addressing world leaders at a U.N. Summit in June 2008, it would cost the world $30 billion to feed the world's 862 million hungry people. (http://www.fao.org/Newsroom/common/ecg/1000853/en/diouf_en.pdf) According to the U.S. Census Bureau, Americans spent a total of $31.9 billion in December,

2004 at retail department stores. (http://www.census.gov/
Press-Release/www/releases/archives/facts for features
special editions/005870.html) What Americans spent on one
Christmas would be enough to solve the world's hunger problems. Think about it.

Furthermore, greed not only leaves many wanting, but it
destroys our relationships.

The biblical writer James states, "*What causes fights and quarrels
among you? Don't they come from your desires that battle within you?
You want something but don't get it. You kill and covet, but you cannot
have what you want. You quarrel and fight...*" (James 4:1-2 NIV).

Financial issues crumble family stability. Why? It usually
comes down to greed. A spouse wants something, and the other
spouse doesn't agree, so an argument ensues. Without reconcilia-
tion over the matter, tension develops in the relationship.

I've stood with family members by the casket of a loved one
as we wept and cried together over their loss. A month later I
found myself counseling them through the anger at the unfair
inheritance they received or the relic someone else received that
was supposed to be theirs. The book of James concludes that the
reason fights and quarrels come among us is because of greed and
the desire to accumulate. We want more and more—and therefore, we fight for it.

Greed corrupts the workplace. For instance, a woman wants
another job or position, so she speaks mistruths to destroy a co-
worker's credibility. Then she fights for what she wants while

leaving others wounded in her trail. Greed will stop at nothing to get what it wants. Greed isolates a person, as does every other sin. It destroys the most vital relationships in one's life.

Greed also destroys an individual's capacity to trust God. In Hebrews 11:6, the author states, *"And without faith it is impossible to please God."* There just isn't any possibility of satisfying God without faith. The scripture writer goes on to say, *"Anyone who comes to Him must believe that He exists and that He rewards those who earnestly seek Him."* (NIV)

What does it mean to have faith? Simply, faith means trusting in God. I trust that God will provide for me and take care of me when I lay my life in His hands. Greed counters that. It makes me self-sufficient instead of God-sufficient. It insists, "It is all up to me. With a little more I can solve my problems." In this I am no longer dependent on the Lord, but distrusting of His ways. And so, where there's distrust in a relationship, there's a breakdown in it. Thus, greed separates us from our most faithful adviser and provider, God Himself.

The Lord has also entrusted us to care for one another. But stinginess hardens our hearts and causes us to ignore the concerns of others. We are fully content to neglect or even sabotage the lives of others as long as our bank accounts, garages, and pantries are filled. Greed is focused on one person and one person only. ME.

Identify

If you find yourself pursuing the accumulation of things, as well as feeling indifference for the needs of others, maybe selfishness has distracted you and handicapped your faith.

Materialism misdirects love. Passion turns from what is actually meaningful to objects that are incapable of giving or receiving affection. Stuff becomes more important than people, even family. Collections, power and prestige become the greedy person's priorities. But in the end, when he or she stands before the throne of Christ, the greedy person will find none of those possessions of any value.

Dante, in *The Divine Comedy*, illustrated hell for the greedy. Its victims were tied face-down to the ground and their backs to heaven for eternity. Because they spent their lives in love with the things of earth and missed out on the things of God, their punishment fit their crime. Greediness misdirected them.

Greed also fears the future. A person cannot appreciate the value of today due to anxiety over what is to come. There develops an all-consuming desire to accumulate enough for the unforeseen. No joy is allowed today because tomorrow may be insufficient. This fear leads to a restless heart.

The wilderness-wanderings of the Israelites detailed in the book of Exodus illustrate the state of a people whose hearts could never be satisfied. The delivered nation began to grumble about having nothing to eat, claiming they should go back to Egypt where they would be better off. God was aware of their concerns and responded with a plan: "Every morning when you get up, there is going to be bread in the dew, called manna. Everyday there will be enough manna so you may gather all you need for that day." His instructions were specific; the Israelites were to collect all they needed for one day. Except the day before the sabbath, in which case, they would collect double. God was teaching His people to trust Him. He promised that when they got up each morning, the bread would be provided.

Moses instructed the people that no one was to keep any of this manna until morning. However, some of them paid no attention and kept part of it until the next day. In the morning they found it was full of maggots and beginning to smell. Moses was understandably angry with them. Their disobedience and miserliness was a sign they did not trust God to provide again tomorrow. God used the manna to teach His people they could trust Him to meet their needs daily. However, in their greed, they distrusted.

Greed says, "I have to hoard it. I have to keep it. It has to be mine. I can't let go of it because if I do, I may not have what I need tomorrow."

I'm not talking about being a wise steward so you have something to fall back on. But when greed enters your life, you're not trusting God but trusting in yourself. In other words, the problem arises when you trust your own resources instead of God's.

If this has ever happened in your life, then you have tasted greed. If you have ever found it difficult giving away something you didn't need to someone who did, then you have tasted greed.

Suppose you've seen a man whose greatest need is a coat. By whatever circumstance he happened to come to your house when he needed a coat, so you went into your closet and found that you had five coats of differing styles and varieties. One particular coat you have had for so long without wearing it that it seems the sensible choice to give away. But then something inside of you says, "But this coat is special to me."

Perhaps you wore this coat at some special occasion, or perhaps someone special bought it for you. Somehow it holds some sort of value. It is important to you. Yet, in front of you stands a man who needs a coat, and you have five. But you struggle to give away something you don't need to someone who needs it. If you have ever faced that feeling, it was greed.

We live in a society of abundance where most of us have all we will ever want. Yet greed whispers, "I cannot give it up because I might lose out."

Let's try to understand Jesus' perspective on the issue. Luke 12:13–14 says, *"Then someone called from the crowd, 'Teacher, please tell my brother to divide our father's estate with me.' Jesus replied, 'Friend, who made me a judge over you to decide such things as that?'"* (NLT).

Now consider the situation. A man came to Jesus and was upset because he was not getting the portion of what was owed to him. He said to Jesus, "Jesus, You are a rabbi. You are wise; take care of this issue." But Jesus took the matter deeper because he realized the man's true issue was not about legalities. Jesus recognized that it was really a greed issue. In verse 15, Jesus said: "*Beware! Guard against every kind of greed. Life is not measured by how much you own.*"

In the New Testament, the word *life* has two distinct meanings. The first is *bio*, which means eating, breathing, living biology. However, the life that Jesus speaks of here is *Zoe*, which is your spiritual God-life or the life God puts in you. Jesus indicated that greed will steal away your God-life. It suffocates that life because you choose not to trust Him anymore. You've put Him aside, and He's no longer a priority.

Jesus continued His point with this example. He said, "*A rich man had a fertile farm that produced fine crops. He said to himself, 'What should I do? I don't have room for all my crops.' Then he said, 'I know! I'll tear down my barns and build bigger ones. Then I'll have room enough to store all my wheat and other goods. And I'll sit back and say to myself, 'My friend, you have enough stored away for years to come. Now take it easy! Eat, drink, and be merry!' But God said to him, 'You fool! You will die this very night. Then who will get everything you worked for?' Yes, a person is a fool to store up earthly wealth but not have a rich relationship with God*" Luke 12:16–21 (NLT).

This man had done very well. He was a good farmer. He knew the land, he knew how to till the ground, and he knew how to plant crops. In fact, he did so well he had to figure out what to do with it all. The important thing to notice is who he consulted about what to do with the excess. *Himself!* He thought to himself,

I've got all this stuff, so what will I do with it? He didn't go to his buddy with whom he had a relationship or to a business partner. He talked to himself because he likely had pushed everyone else away with his greed. Jesus was saying this man is empty and had missed the true meaning of life.

In his abundance, the rich man ignored the needs of those around him. This man had plenty, but he couldn't care less for those who didn't. Eventually, the man comes up with the great idea of tearing down his barns to build bigger ones. He doesn't stop to think of taking care of the needy, even though he has enough to last him for a long time. Instead, his solution was to build bigger barns.

What we tear down and what we build up reflects a lot about what's going on in our lives. If we make a commitment to God to tear down the greed in our lives and to build back generosity, it says a lot about what is in us. This man tore down the little bit of greed he had, but he built back more greed.

Test yourself on this: whenever you have extra money, what is the first thought of what you will do with it? Maybe you pay the car off. You ask yourself, "What will I do now? Buy another one?" Perhaps you received a bonus. You have a little extra. So will you go get yourself something, or use the extra to benefit others? What you tear down and what you build back up has a lot to say about you.

This man said, "Tear down the small barns and build bigger barns," and now he had enough stored away for years to come.

He could simply take it easy—eat, drink, and be merry. Maybe he deserved retirement. There is nothing at all wrong with retirement. It's a good thing. But the issue here is that this man had the ability to grow crops, to make more money and to help others. However, in retirement, he moved to Florida, got a condo and played golf. He could have looked over his society and said, "I tell you what, you don't have enough to eat, so I will teach you to farm. I made my living at it and did well." He could have said, "I will take the abilities I have, and I will help you." Instead of giving a man a fish, he could have taught a man *to* fish. Rather, he said, "It's about me and only me."

Let's consider what Jesus said about it. He certainly wasn't easy on greed; He didn't brush it off. Instead, in His parable, God said, *"You fool! You will die this very night. Then who will get everything you worked for?"*

Greed fools its victim. It offers a false sense of satisfaction and comfort.

Jesus continued, *"Yes, a person is a fool to store up earthly wealth, but not have a rich relationship with God."* He illustrated that the man had exchanged a relationship with God for a little bit of stuff. It's like giving up a million dollars in exchange for a penny.

Deliver

So how do we become delivered from greed's deadly grip?

Remember I said in the introduction that the Ten Commandments are not the Ten Options, and that they were given by God to protect His people. One of the commandments says remember the Sabbath day and keep it holy. God established the Sabbath day to teach His people they can trust Him. The Lord taught, "Work six days, but trust that I will turn that six into seven; I will meet your needs if you put me first. So remember the Sabbath day and keep it holy." In other words, spend a day to enjoy your family, your God, your environment, and the good things God has given you.

Take a break and recognize that you can work six days, and God will take care of you. The Sabbath is a reminder that you can trust God. Greed will not want you to take a sabbath. Greed will want you to say, "No, no, no, I've got to work more so I can have more. I've got to pay for what I have, and I've got to pay for the more I want." Greed convinces you to not give up any opportunity to get more.

I work on the Sabbath myself; some people say preachers work only one day a week. Well, that's not true, but I am here every Sunday. I work on the Sabbath, so I have to take a sabbath on another day during the week.

For years, I worked in the ministry and never took a day off. Why? I had something to prove. I had to prove to all the naysayers that preachers do work on more than just Sunday. It was a pride issue. I had to prove that I could do it, that I could excel, that I could do better and that my church could grow faster. It would happen because I worked every day of the week, and I worked hard.

One day God said to me, "This is a sin. You have to take a sabbath because it is a day for saying, 'God, I am leaving it all—my needs, my desires, my schedule, my reputation—all of it up to You. You are my greatest need. Take care of the rest. I trust you.'"

If we're going to overcome greed, you and I have to become respectful of the Holy Sabbath day, and proclaim "I don't have to work because, God, You will take care of it all."

Second, we need to understand ownership.

James 1:17 says, *"Every good and perfect gift is from above, coming down from the Father of the heavenly lights, who does not change like the shifting shadows"* (NIV). Everything we have comes from God. Imagine a world where every fruit was an apple or every color was blue. God gave us a world filled with variety. He gave it to us to enjoy; He blessed us with it. Just take a moment to think of all the things God has given you in the past 24 hours. He has given air to breath, food to eat, friends to be around, a church to worship in, a house to live in—all of that is from God. Be thankful for them.

Greed would take those for granted, saying, "Those are not privileges; those are my rights. I deserve them." But greed can be conquered when you and I recognize that all of our blessings are from God.

Since God is the provider of all things good in our lives, how does He expect us to use them? Jesus told a rich young ruler that he could not be Jesus's disciple without giving up everything he owned. I've read that before and thought, *Jesus, do You mean everything? Are You talking about the whole list? Because if a person gives up everything, how will he or she survive? And if all Your followers give up everything the people who don't give up everything will be the only people who have anything. Is that really what You mean?*

NO! Jesus is saying that giving up everything is transferring ownership. It was His in the beginning. He gave it to you. Now He wants you to offer it back to Him. If you will overcome greed, you need to come to a point in your life where you can say, "God it's all Yours. This car is Yours. If You want to use it for Your glory, do it. This house is Yours. If You want to use it to build relationships, then do it. The money, the food, the stuff-all of it is Yours. Do with it what you want. I give up my rights to it; You're now the owner."

When we transfer ownership to God, our attachments lose their grip, and our concern becomes using our resources in a way that pleases God.

Have you ever borrowed somebody else's car? When you do you don't treat it the same way you treat your own. Usually if you borrow someone's car you don't squeal the tires and you drive carefully. You may care for it in a different way than you might your own. You care for it in a way that you'll be proud to return it to its rightful owner. This is just an example of the change of outlook you have when your assets belongs to God.

If you get to the point where everything you have is not yours but God's, then you will begin to look at your belongings differently. Your things will be God's to use however He wants to use them. You can let go of greed when you begin to understand who owns everything you have.

The last essential thing to do in order to get rid of greed is to practice generosity. Generosity is the antibiotic for the deadly disease of greed. Learn to become generous.

Tithing teaches us generosity. The tithe we give to a church is not just to pay the preacher's salary. God established tithing to keep us from being greedy. Malachi 3:10 reads, *"Bring the whole tithe into the storehouse, so that there may be food in My house, and test Me now in this,' says the LORD of hosts, 'if I will not open for you the windows of heaven and pour out for you a blessing until it overflows'"* (NASB).

But we should not only practice generosity at church. It is meant to be lived out in all areas of our lives. Paul said in 1 Timothy 6:17-19, *"Command those who are rich in this present world not to be arrogant nor to put their hope in wealth, which is so uncertain, but to put their hope in God. Command them to do good, to be rich in good deeds, and to be generous and willing to share. In this way they will lay up treasure for themselves as a firm foundation for the coming age, so that they may take hold of the life that is truly life"* (NIV).

You'll note that he said *those who are rich*. You may say, "I'm really not 'rich'; you should see my bank account." But in

2 Corinthians 8 and 9, he said that even those who were poor gave out of their poverty. *"Out of the most severe trial, their overflowing joy and their extreme poverty welled up in rich generosity"* (2 Corinthians 8:2 NIV). If you live in America, you are rich compared to others. So, when he says *in your wealth*, don't become big-headed. Don't get all puffed up, and don't think that you're somebody because, in reality, your wealth is uncertain. On September 29, 2008, what happened on Wall Street? About 1.2 trillion dollars crashed, vanished. Jesus said do not put your investments in things that moth and rust will destroy. Put them in eternal things. Put your hope in God. Be rich in heavenly values. Don't be puffed up, and don't look at stuff as your security, but do enjoy everything God has provided for you. Be thankful for it while you have it, but don't attach yourself to it.

That is a point that I don't want you to miss in this book. We could talk about greed and feel that we have to get rid of all of our stuff because we can't enjoy these things. But that's not the case *because* God has blessed us with things, and He wants us to enjoy them. But He also wants a part of that enjoyment to be about how you use what you have to help others.

In 1 Timothy 6 Paul went on to say, *"Command them to do good."* That is, make a wise investment with your generosity. He continued, *"to be rich in good deeds, and to be generous and willing to share."* That means be excited about sharing. There are daily opportunities to do something nice for someone else. Paul said that when they were *"willing to share"* they laid up *"treasure for themselves as a firm foundation for the coming age, so that they may take hold of the life that is truly life."* If you want to invest in the here and now, invest in things that will not fade away. Invest in the things of heaven. When you and I become generous, we start to kill the greed in our lives.

Here's a homework assignment for you involving money. I want you to think about what fits in your budget. It could be 5, 10, 20, 50, or 100 dollars; whatever works. This week give away whatever amount you just decided. If you've got kids, get them to be a part of giving it away, too. When you go to a restaurant and see people — and you don't even have to know them — tell the waiter that you want to pick up their lunch tab. Don't tell the people who paid and just walk out. Or hand money to the guy you pass on the street. Or give money to somebody you work with, or give it to somebody at school. Just be a blessing to somebody. Give away the amount that you set this week.

Two things will happen when you do this. When you let go of that money, it will reveal if you have some greed issues in your life. You'll know because stinginess will well up in you. It may just be a small amount of money, but the sacrifice will reveal the attachment to it. Try it and see how it works out.

Second, and most importantly, this money will let you experience the joy of giving. It will put a smile on your face. I guarantee, it will make your heart a little bit warmer than when you started. Being generous will bring so much joy, it will take you to a new level. Greed says, "Oh, you can't afford to be generous because if you're generous, then you won't have enough for yourself." Yet, God says that you will reap what you sow; it is more of a blessing to give than to receive.

Finally, if you're going to change, you have to admit that greediness is a problem. For some people this is going to be a hard one, but you'll have to say, "God, I'm greedy, and I have a problem with that. I ask that You forgive me and help me to become generous, so I can lose the grip of greed in my life."

LUST

*T*hen God said, *"Let us make human beings in our image, to be like us. They will reign over the fish in the sea, the birds in the sky, the livestock, all the wild animals on the earth, and the small animals that scurry along the ground." So God created human beings in his own image. In the image of God he created them; male and female he created them. Then God blessed them and said, "Be fruitful and multiply. Fill the earth and govern it. Reign over the fish in the sea, the birds in the sky, and all the animals that scurry along the ground." Then God said, "Look! I have given you every seed-bearing plant throughout the earth and all the fruit trees for your food. And I have given every green plant as food for all the wild animals, the birds in the sky, and the small animals that scurry along the ground — everything that has life." And that is what happened. Then God looked over all he made, and he saw that it was very good! And evening passed and morning came, marking the sixth day* (Genesis 1:26-31 NLT).

Of everything God created — the mountains, the sky, the sea, the animals — only once did God say, "Let us make this in our image." That one thing was mankind. Scripture says He formed men and women in His likeness, so that they might display His characteristics on this earth. God created and loves all people. Therefore, all people have a special place in His heart. In an individual's most perfect state of being, he or she reflects the glory of the Almighty God to others.

The second thing we learn from this scripture is that procreation is God's idea. Verse 28 says, *"Then God blessed them,"* referring to man and woman. The blessing actually began with a command, *"Be fruitful and multiply. Fill the earth...."* So God created, ordained, and yes, blessed the sexual relationship of male and female from the beginning. Sex is God's idea. In God's order, within the boundaries of the covenant of marriage, it is a good thing.

The real and exciting truth we learn from this chapter in the Bible is that God loves all people, God created all people, and sex was God's idea.

In fact, scripture teaches that the body and the soul are one; you can't separate the two. Understanding this fact lays important groundwork for understanding why lust is such a problem.

Let's look at this New Testament passage, which says, *"May God himself, the God of peace, sanctify you through and through. May your whole spirit, soul and body, be kept blameless at the coming of our Lord Jesus Christ"* (1 Thessalonians 5:23 NIV).

This scripture, along with others, declares a believer may be sanctified wholly. That sanctification includes the body and the soul. You may ask, "What does that have to do with the concept of lust?" A lot. The sin of lust believes precisely the opposite of sanctification.

First, the sin of lust does not view people as created in the image of God or as individuals valued and loved by Him. Lust looks at people as objects of desire to be pursued and overcome. Second, lust takes the gift of sex that God invented and distorts it from everything He intended it to be. Finally, lust believes that the body can be separated from the soul. In other words, we can have sexual relations outside the boundaries of God's design and it's okay because it's just physical, not really having anything to do with God. Therefore, it isn't a problem.

So is promiscuity seriously a problem? What does the addiction of lust look like in our society? According to Jerry Ropelato, founder and Chief Executive Officer of TopTenREVIEWS,Inc., in only one year the pornography industry in the United States amasses over 13 billion dollars of revenue. This amount is more than the NFL and major league baseball made combined last year (www.plunkerttresearch.com/Industries/sports/sportsstatistics/tab id/273/default.aspx) (http://money.cnn.com/2007/10/25/commentary/sportsbiz/index.htm).

It gets worse. The National Coalition for the Protection of Children and Families (NCPCF) claims that approximately 40 million people in the United States are sexually involved in the Internet. Over 100,000 websites offer illegal child pornography, and of the 13 billion dollars that American's spent on pornography last year, 3 billion dollars was spent on child pornography. An estimated 90% of eight- to 16-year-olds have been exposed to pornography online, most of the time while doing their homework. The average age of a child when he or she is first exposed to Internet pornography, in the United States, is age 11. And 20% of men admit to accessing pornography at work along with 13% of women.

According to Peggy Vaughan, the author of *The Monogamy Myth*, conservative infidelity statistics estimate that 60% of all men and 40% of all women in the United States will have an extra-marital affair, and that 20% of the marriages in America will end in divorce because of infidelity.

Lust is a pandemic problem which affects the families of America. In every way possible, Satan tries to destroy the good things in our lives. He works to sabotage our families, our marriages, our jobs, our future, etc. And he uses lust to do it.

Remember the story of King David? Throughout his life he authored many psalms, and the Bible called him a man after God's own heart. But after his affair with Bathsheba, his family became divided, and, eventually, so did his kingdom. This erosion can be traced back to the day David stood on the palace roof and lusted.

Why is lust so deadly? And how has it become so rampant? Simply, we've trivialized the problem.

Galatians 5:19 states, *"When you follow the desires of your sinful nature, the results are very clear: sexual immorality, impurity, lustful pleasures"* (NLT).

In the King James translation of this verse, two words are very clear, *adultery* and *uncleanness*. Study reveals that the first of all six sexual immoralities in the Greek is described by the word *pornea*. *Pornea* means sexual activity outside of marriage, and it covers both adultery and homosexuality. Now if you take the word *pornea* and put it into the feminine, it becomes *porneous,* which is a word used to describe a prostitute. This is saying that if a woman commits adultery, she is acting as a prostitute. That doesn't necessarily mean she had sex for money. She may have given over her heart, her passions or desires. Nevertheless, she sold herself. This is the way God is describing it in these verses. For a man, the word is *pornea,* which means sexual relationships with a prostitute. God is ramping this issue up and saying that your culture may say it's acceptable and okay, but it's sin.

You've probably already figured this out, but the word *porneas* is the source of the word *pornography.* If *pornea* is about prostitution, and *grafting* refers to the writing of something, then *pornography is* the writings of a prostitute. Scripture is telling us that pornography is mental prostitution. This is serious business in God's eyes.

At the start of this book, we looked at the scripture John 10:10. *"The thief comes only to steal and kill and destroy; I have come that they may have life, and have it to the full"* (NIV). Jesus said that the thief, Satan, comes *only* to destroy our lives. The "only" part is exactly what I want to talk about. You must realize that Satan doesn't want to make you feel better about yourself or help you in any way. He has one desire, and one desire only—to destroy everything good in your life and in mine.

The sin of lust has the same goal; Satan uses it as a foothold in your life to do one thing and one thing only — to destroy you. He wants to destroy your mind, your closest relationships and your reputation. He wants to break up your marriage, and he wants to add shame to your life. And eventually, these kinds of issues left unaddressed and uncontrolled could lead to problems such as child abuse or rape. It's a slippery slope.

When a person takes cocaine for the first time, there is a part of the brain that triggers an addiction. After just one hit of cocaine, a person will want it again in a desperate way. The same thing that's triggered in the brain when taking cocaine is triggered when you and I look at pornography. In other words, we cannot just look at it once.

Identify

Lust wants to steal, kill, and destroy everything good in our lives; and it is as deadly as cocaine. So let's identify it. We need to take an internal look at ourselves.

First, lust is self-love. It could almost be called sexual greed. Lust has one desire: self-fulfillment. Relationally, that desire is to dominate or to control another. When sexual desire becomes the dominant factor in a relationship, it's turned into lust. Thomas Aquinas said that lust is like a lion pursuing a deer. All the lion sees is a tasty meal, good for the lion and bad for the deer. Lust is focused only on itself, its own selfish desires, and its own satisfaction.

Second, lust is dehumanizing. When we look at another person as a prize to obtain or to conquer it belittles God's creation. We don't look at the person as good and valuable. Instead, we look at the person for what he or she can do to benefit us, and it's at that point the relationship becomes lust. God looks at a person and says, "This is someone I love. This is someone for whom I gave My Son. This is a body and a soul and a spirit." In lust, we look at an individual as someone merely to have.

Third, lust is unwilling to commit. Lust is there for as long as the pleasure is there, and then it's gone. True love commits to a relationship throughout the good and the bad. True love stands in front of others and says, "I love this person so much that I want you to know about it. I will wear a ring to display that I'm committed to this person. If I wake up tomorrow and things are not going my way, it doesn't matter; I'm still committed to this person." On the other hand, lust says, "As long as I'm satisfied and happy, then we're together. But when things get tough, I'm out the door." Lust is never willing to commit. It remains as long as its needs are met. It is temporary, short-lived.

Matthew 5:27-30 says, *"You have heard that it was said, 'Do not commit adultery.' But I tell you that anyone who looks at a woman lustfully has already committed adultery with her in his heart. If your right eye causes you to sin, gouge it out and throw it away. It is better for you to lose one part of your body than for your whole body to be thrown into hell. And if your right hand causes you to sin, cut if off and throw it away. It is better for you to lose one part of your body than for your whole body to go into hell"* (NIV).

I wish Jesus had simply told us to put on blinders or dark sunglasses. In this scripture, Jesus said you've heard the Ten Commandments, so don't commit adultery. Further, He taught that lust accompanies destruction. Jesus was very straightforward, saying that if you've committed lust, you're in danger of the fires of hell. In fact, He said it's better to pull your own eye out than to look at a person lustfully. A wise man would rather trade his eye than have to spend eternity in hell. Jesus taught that lewdness corrupts. Don't walk its path. Certainly you and I are smart enough to figure out precautionary solutions without having to cut off an arm or gouge out an eye. Perhaps dark glasses would be a simpler solution. Just don't look.

Deliver

Jesus' point is reiterated throughout scripture. Its wisdom directs us to deliverance. Let's search for its wise counsel in this matter.

First we must run from temptation.

It worked for Joseph in the Old Testament. We read there about Joseph who had been thrown into slavery and at the time of this account was working in the house of Potiphar, a leader in the government. Joseph must have been a pretty fine-looking fellow because Potiphar's wife had her eye on him and liked what she saw. One day when Joseph went into the house to attend to his duties, none of the other servants were around. Potiphar's wife caught him by his cloak and told him to come to bed with her. But instead, he left his cloak in her hands and ran out of the house. Like a flash of lightening, he was out of there. When temptation arose, he ran from it. He fled. Too bad more people don't simply run. Way too often we fall short when it comes to lust because we set ourselves up for it rather than fleeing it.

Take a lesson from Joseph. Don't set yourself up. Run from lust as fast as you can. You know people you shouldn't hang out with and places you shouldn't go to and what Internet sites you shouldn't visit. Run!

Today one of the best things you can say is, "I need to make some adjustments in my life. I need to put myself in a position so I won't be tempted in the area of lust." If you are married and already in a relationship where you find yourself sharing personal information about your spouse with someone of the opposite sex, you're skating on thin ice. You can have an emotional affair just as well as you can have a physical affair. If you're at that place, then you need to run from it. This is a serious issue. It will destroy you. I say it again—run from it.

Next, you need to view each person as God does. He or she is not just someone there for your pleasure. When you see a person, realize that he or she has a home, a family, a mom and a dad. Consider this a person whom God loves very much and for whom Jesus died. Start to look at others and see them the way that God sees them.

"Do you not know that your body is a temple of the Holy Spirit, who is in you, whom you have received from God? You are not your own; you were bought at a price. Therefore honor God with your body" (NIV), 1 Corinthians 6:19-20 says. This scripture tells us *you* are so valuable that Jesus paid the ultimate price for you; death on a cross. But He *also* did it for the woman in the magazine, and for the guy who lives in your neighborhood, and for your co-worker. He did it for all of them because they are also valuable to Him. Lust dehumanizes a person to the point that he or she is just an object. Begin to look at people as God does.

Third, find someone in your life to whom you may be accountable.

After King David committed adultery, Nathan the prophet told him a story. We find it in 2 Samuel 12. Nathan told about a man in the kingdom who was taken advantage of and had a lamb stolen from him. This infuriated David. He got really heated up saying, "What do you mean? How could someone take advantage of another in this manner?" Nathan insisted this was the case, and David declared that something must be done to the thief. But then Nathan looked David straight in the eye and said, "You are the man." David had sinned with Bathsheba, a married woman, and fallen out of bounds from where he needed to be with God.

We all need someone in our lives who loves us and can speak to us just that straight. We don't need someone who looks down his or her nose at us and says, "I'm better than you." We need a person in our lives who wants the best for us, but can also look us in the eye and tell us when we have a problem.

The realm of lust is normally a secret obsession that we don't want anyone else knowing. One of the actions we need to take is to get honest with ourselves and get honest with others.

Another action is to plan precautionary measures ahead of time, before the temptation arises. There are many filters you can put on your computer at home or at work to stop your looking at obscene content on the Internet. I've witnessed multiple families ripped apart and lives ruined as a result of pornography. It is important to build these safeguards into your life. Sin and lust are powerful and can overtake your blessings.

Finally, we have to seek help and forgiveness from God. I'll include a portion here of what David wrote in Psalm 51 after being confronted with his sin.

"Create in me a pure heart, O God,
and renew a steadfast spirit within me.
Do not cast me from your presence
or take your Holy Spirit from me.
Restore to me the joy of your salvation
and grant me a willing spirit, to sustain me"
(Psalm 51:10-12 NIV).

David said, "Lord, I've messed up, and I need Your help." That might be the prayer you need to pray today. Maybe you need to admit, "God I've messed up, and I need Your help with this. I need You to cleanse me because I can't do it myself. I've tried to many times, and I've failed many times. God, I've talked to You often, but I'm coming to You fresh and new today. I need You."

Isaiah 1:18 says, *"'Come now, let us reason together,' says the Lord. 'Though your sins are like scarlet, they shall be as white as snow; though they are red as crimson, they shall be like wool'"* (NIV). This is one verse of many in the Bible telling us that our sins can be cleansed.

Lust is a sin, but it's not an unforgiveable sin. Lust is a terrible addiction that takes you inside yourself. It makes you think no one else would understand and that even God wouldn't care. It will cause you to question whether there's any hope for you and if things could get any worse. These are lies from Satan, who wants to destroy your life and your relationship with God.

This sin can be forgiven. God can clean you up. It takes honest confession. Obedience to His Spirit can deliver you from the addiction of lust. He has the power to change you.

You might be reading this book today knowing far too well the damage of sexual sin. Somewhere along your life's journey, you may have been affected by it. Somebody did something out of lust that he or she shouldn't have done. Right this very minute God can clean you up, and He can fill up the emptiness and make you whole. He can heal the hurt. I know that God is powerful enough, loving enough and caring enough to want to heal you when you hurt.

We can't look at 13 billion dollars spent a year, children victimized, and homes destroyed and say that this is not a subject we need to address. God not only wants us to address it because it is sin and it will send many to hell, but because God wants good for our lives. Jesus said, "I came that they may have life and have it abundantly" (John 10:10 NASB).

GLUTTONY

Ever since I was a kid, I've loved doughnuts. When I was young, I would go to the doughnut shop, and the owner knew me so well she would make peanut butter long johns just for me. So when I heard Krispy Kreme Doughnuts was opening near my home, I didn't know how I would contain myself. I waited for weeks anticipating the grand opening.

Krispy Kreme doughnuts are amazing. The restaurant is like a factory, having a conveyor belt that transports the doughnuts through the cooking process. It always reminds me of a treadmill. Kind of ironic, huh? I've thought, *Let that doughnut run through one more time; take the calories right out of it.* When the shop finally opened, I wasted no time; I bought my dozen and headed home. I ate one, and man — I don't think I had ever tasted a doughnut so delicious, so I ate another one. In that 20-minute ride home, I ate nine doughnuts. As I pulled into the driveway, I was certain I never wanted to see another Krispy Kreme doughnut for the rest of my life. I was sick, and I learned the valuable lesson that too much of a good thing can make you ill.

Gluttony is about excess—about too much. The first gluttons are found in Genesis 3, where we read the story of Adam and Eve. In the last chapter of this book, we looked at this story of

God's original design in relation to lust. Now we'll look at the fall of Adam and Eve when they chose to disobey God.

Genesis 3:1–6 says, *"The serpent was the shrewdest of all the wild animals the Lord God had made. One day he asked the woman, 'Did God really say that you must not eat the fruit from any of the trees in the garden?'*

"'Of course we may eat fruit from the trees in the garden,' the woman replied. 'It's only the fruit from the tree in the middle of the garden that we are not allowed to eat. God said, 'You must not eat of it or even touch it; if you do, you will die.''

"'You won't die!' the serpent replied to the woman. 'God knows that your eyes will be opened as soon as you eat it, and you will be like God, knowing both good and evil.'

"The woman was convinced. She saw that the tree was beautiful and its fruit looked delicious, and she wanted the wisdom it would give her. So she took some of the fruit and ate it. Then she gave some to her husband, who was with her, and he ate it, too. At that moment their eyes were opened, and they suddenly felt shame at their nakedness. So they sewed fig leaves together to cover themselves" (NLT).

Isn't it interesting that the temptation which started the fall of mankind was about *food?* God had given them specific instructions about what was best for them. He had provided all their needs and even walked with them in the evening. Adam and Eve had stayed away from the tree of knowledge of good and evil because He had told them to. The newly-created humans didn't really need to eat that fruit, because they lacked nothing. Just imagine what the Garden looked like and all the lushness that was there. Every fruit and vegetable God had created was at their disposal. There was no shortage of God's blessings. The forbidden tree of knowledge of good and evil was excess.

There are many points of discussion that go along with this story, but the "I want more" or "I want what God's not giving me" attitude of Adam and Eve leads us straight to gluttony. Their actions implied, "I'm not happy enough with what I have. God's holding out on me. I want more." Adam and Eve could have brought their questions to God concerning the forbidden fruit and the wisdom they felt they lacked. However, instead of turning to Him, they focused on the fruit and gave into temptation. In other words, they wanted more than they actually needed and they resorted to their own means of getting it.

Early in church history, gluttony was placed at the top of the deadly-sin list. In that culture, the vast majority of people lived in poverty and scrounged around for very little food. Yet there were people who had much wealth. Some wealthier citizens gorged themselves on food, while many poor went hungry altogether.

Even in the United States, we have a 30% obesity rate while there are 1.4 billion of the world's population living on less than $1.25 a day. We live in a culture where we have so much, and yet every six seconds in our world a child will die of malnutrition or related causes. (http://www.globalissues.org/article/4/poverty-around-the-world; http://www.wfp.org/hunger/stats).

We're bombarded with food. We live in excess, and that excess is affecting us. The rise of obesity in the United States over the past 20 years is dramatic. Obesity is a major contributor to heart disease, diabetes and some types of cancer. (http://www.cdc.gov/obesity/data/trends.html). It's a tragedy because the sin of gluttony destroys our bodies.

But not only that, the way we eat affects how we feel and function throughout our days. Dr. Gary Smalley, founder of the Smalley Relationship Center and author of the book *Food and Love*, claims that "foods high in fat, sugar, and chemical additives may contribute to a host of negative emotions, while foods rich in nutrients—fresh fruits and vegetables, grains and lean meats—may contribute to positive emotions." Further, he continues, "if people exhibit uncontrolled anger, pessimism, anxiety, or bad moods on a regular basis, their relationships are bound to be affected. People with these emotional traits will be more likely to have conflicts with their spouses, children and even co-workers. On the other hand, if people are generally ruled by joy, peace, patience and a positive attitude, their relationships are bound to be stronger." Simply put, Dr. Smalley writes, "you *feel* what you eat." [Dr. Gary Smalley, *Food and Love (Wheaton: Tyndale House, 2001) 19, 20, 37]*

So if eating excessive junk food makes you feel junky, then that will likely affect your responses to others; and your actions and reactions to others affect your relationships. Satan knows that if you don't feel well, you are distracted from God's kingdom-building work. And if you are crabby, he may use that to tear down the kingdom. Gluttony keeps us from being effective and from being the ministers God wants us to be. It also holds us back from enjoying the life God has intended for us. Once again, we see how sin isolates us from others.

The real challenge is that food is an obsession in American culture. According to Eric Schlosser, author of *Fast Food Nation*, Americans spent $110 billion on fast food alone in 2001, more than they spent on books, magazines, CDs and movies put together. (http://www.cbsnews.com/stories/2002/01/31/health/main326858.shtml) A whole television network completely dedicated to food airs with 76 different cooking shows. Have a look in your yellow pages and count the restaurants listed. This in itself highlights the obsession we have with food. In a culture where so much is available to us, gluttony can be a great temptation.

As I searched the scriptures on this topic, I didn't find anything that says food is a bad thing. In fact, in the Garden of Eden, God had blessed Adam and Eve with many good foods. Even Jesus, when He came to this earth, enjoyed a good meal. The Pharisees accused Jesus of being a glutton, as shown in Matthew 11:19, where it says, *"The Son of Man came eating and drinking, and they say, 'Here is a glutton and a drunkard, a friend of tax collectors and sinners.'..."* (NIV). When Jesus came to earth, He healed the blind and the lame, but He also chose to feed 5,000 people their lunch. His first miracle, involving wine, took place at a wedding feast. Jesus enjoyed food, especially with friends. One of the sacraments we enjoy in church is based on food—the Lord's Supper, in memory of His last meal with His disciples. And the Bible also says when we die and go to heaven, or when Jesus returns—whichever happens first—we shall all sit around a great banquet table and enjoy the marriage supper of the Lamb and His church. The Bible doesn't imply in any way that food is bad.

Food was given to mankind for nourishment. The fact that God created so many nutrients and flavors in the different varieties of plants, tells us that God also intended us to enjoy His food. However, when food is used outside of God's design, it becomes unhealthful. The Lord wants what's best for us. Think about it; research has shown that raw fruits and vegetables and whole grains are more nutritious than cooked and processed foods. That's not a new discovery for God. He planned it all along.

"The Lord God commanded the man, saying 'From any tree of the garden you may eat freely'" (Genesis 2:16 NASB).

God cares about our health. That's why He was so strict with the Israelites, His representatives to the world. Leviticus 11 records God's specific instructions on which meats they were to eat and which they were to avoid. For the New Testament church, He spoke through Paul saying, *"Do you not know that you are a temple of God and that the Spirit of God dwells in you? If any man destroys the temple of God, God will destroy him, for the temple of God is holy, and that is what you are"* (1 Corinthians 3:16-17 NASB). The Almighty God has so much respect for your body that He calls it holy and He chooses to dwell with you, in it.

Jesus said, *"Here I am! I stand at the door and knock. If anyone hears my voice and opens the door, I will come in and eat with him, and he with me"* (Revelation 3:20 NIV).

If God respects the well-being of your body and calls it His temple, shouldn't you have the same regard for it? Paul wrote in 1 Corinthians 6:20 to "glorify God in your body" (NASB). What particular actions are you taking today to honor God in your physical body? For some of us it may be time for an overhaul of the temple.

Food is a comfort to people. It satisfies our physical hunger. But unfortunately, many of us misuse food. Our diet was intended to give us physical nourishment. It was never intended to fill up emptiness in our hearts. When we have a spiritual emptiness in our lives, we sometimes want to fill it up with food. But filling up a spiritual emptiness with physical things is like taking penicillin for a broken heart. It just won't work. Only God Himself can satisfy our spirits.

When individuals use food or drink for emotional fulfillment, the comfort lasts only as long as the refreshment is in the mouth—so they return for more, again and again. The result is harmful to the physical body because too much causes imbalance. Even more significantly, the meal has been given power in the person's life that it was not intended to have. Satan jumps on this. His talent is to make things seem as they're not, in order to mislead us away from God. If he can use food—or anything else—to influence people to depend on something other than God, he'll use it.

Infatuation with food, as either entertainment or vice, generally leads to misuse and brings unhealthy consequences to our bodies. The pursuit of more may easily become an unconscious obsession. If we become obsessed with food, it becomes a focal point in our lives; even to the point of idolatry. Paul wrote in Romans 1:21,25: *"For although they knew God, they neither glorified Him as God nor gave thanks to him, but their thinking became futile and their foolish hearts were darkened.... They exchanged the truth of God for a lie, and worshipped and served created things rather than the Creator..."* (NIV).

In the Ten Commandments, it says, *"You shall have no other gods before me."* There should be no one—nothing else—-that can take His place. *"You shall not make for yourself an idol in the form of anything in heaven above or on the earth beneath or in the waters below. You shall not bow down to them or worship them; for I, the Lord your God, am a jealous God..."* (Exodus 20:3-5 NIV). In other words, God is saying He wants complete devotion. He wants to be the only god in your life because He designed you and knows what's best for you. Only He has the ability to fill you completely—physically and spiritually. God clearly states that there's no room for any other idols or gods in your life. He says, "I am to be it. You shall have no other obsessions before Me."

People regularly become obsessed with food, either too much of it or too little of it. While many comfort-feed, others are consumed with the concern of gaining too much weight. Whatever the reason, they become preoccupied with calories and not eating a balanced diet, which often leads to other problems, such as poor nutrition or eating disorders. In a sense, that, too, can become idolatry because it's an obsession with food. It monopolizes their minds and actions. Might we even go as far as describing that too as gluttony? Gluttony is about extremes, imbalance. God's desire for us is health. Health looks different for different people. Perhaps the best definition of gluttony develops either way when food becomes an idol for us.

Many of our perceptions of "health" are mandated by what society calls beauty. How does our culture define what the "perfect person" looks like? Take a look at magazines at the grocery store. If you're a woman, the media at the check-out stand tells you that being beautiful is about being super-thin and tan. Likewise for a man, you must be tan and muscular. According to these magazines, along with the rest of society, this is "perfection."

Ironically, in the 17th century, a painting of a beautiful woman likely displayed a person who was rather round or plump with pale skin. In the 17th century, if you were skinny it was an indication that you didn't have enough resources for the basic essentials of life. If your skin was tan or your body was muscular, it meant you worked outside doing manual labor and you weren't a member of the elite, having servants of your own to work for you. A beautiful person at that time had a very different shape and look than what our culture defines as "beautiful" today.

Culture's advice is not always the best gauge of health. If you are doing everything in your power to become like the women on the magazine covers, realize that God made you unique and His desire for you is wellness and balance.

Gluttony boils down to an obsessive nature. One may even be gluttonous in idols other than food, such as materialism, entertainment, or sports. Anything that becomes all-consuming, causing us to focus on our desires at the risk of our needs, is not safe. God becomes jealous of anything that becomes a crutch before Him.

Identify

To know when something has become an idol in our lives, we must ask some honest questions: What are the sacrifices we've made for it? Do we have the ability to say no to it and walk away when necessary? Is our focus on *what* God has provided rather than God the Provider?

More directly, when we consider our food we should ask ourselves, are we sacrificing our health for it? Are we sacrificing relationships? Are we sacrificing our well-being for the idol of food? If the answer to any of those questions is yes, your compulsion has grown out of proportion and may have turned into gluttony.

Another indicator that food has become an idol in our lives is that it rules our actions. If we cannot pass on the second serving, if we cannot say no to sweets, we likely have lost self-control. And if we have lost control, then who or what is in control? Our cravings for food. Our desires are then taking over and calling the shots in our circumstances. They are dictating our actions. Yet, there should be only One who calls the shots — God. If anything takes the place of God, it is out of place.

Proverbs 25:27–28 says, *"It is not good to eat too much honey, nor is it honorable to seek one's own honor. Like a city whose walls are broken down is a man who lacks self-control"* (NIV). Solomon used food as an illustration to explain that when we lose self-control, we become like a city that no longer has a wall to protect itself from the enemy. The enemy of our soul wants to kill, steal, and destroy; and if he can, then he will use food to do that. When we lose self-control over the area of food, or anything else in our lives, we are giving Satan an access point into our circumstances. When our habits are out of control, we need to release control to God and follow His direction.

Deliver

To help us deal with gluttony, we have to put food in its proper place in our lives. In order to do this, we must first recognize what its proper place is. Food isn't here to control us or to manage our stress; it isn't here to make us happy or to fill our souls. Food is here for nourishment. Keep sustenance in its appropriate rank by thanking God for every bite.

You might have prayed this prayer as a child,

"God is great. God is good.

Thank you for this food. Amen."

This is important because, when you and I are thankful for our food, we're putting it in proper perspective. Sometimes I stop and say, "I recognize, God, this comes from You. This food is not my god; this has been a blessing to me from You. I choose to remember that and be thankful."

Another benefit in thanking God for our food is that we recognize how privileged we are. Just imagine the millions of people around the world who don't have the resources to eat even one meal. You and I can look in our cabinets and, for most of us, they're pretty full. We've got more than we need. Gratitude helps us respect our resources.

The church has offered its own solution for gluttony over the past 2000 years. The discipline of fasting has been corporately practiced traditionally twice a year according to the church calendar: on Advent preceding Christmas, and at Lent preceding Easter.

Why do we fast?

First of all, we fast to sensitize ourselves so we can recognize what God has given us.

Second of all, we fast to focus on self-control. Each year at my church we have an Ash Wednesday service at the start of Lent, during which we're challenged to choose something to fast. This practice helps us exercise self-control in the areas of life where we may have lost control. One of the things I usually choose to fast at Lent is dessert. By about the second week, I find myself dreaming of doughnuts, which is a bad sign with four weeks left to fast. But during those weeks of sacrifice, I'm keenly reminded that I don't need sweets to survive. Though my sweet-tooth usually tells me differently, the tempting delicacies are not something I have to have. Fasting helps strengthen self-control.

Fasting can also help us identify with those who are hungry. How can you and I, in the United States, relate to anyone who has missed meal after meal? After all, as soon as most of us are hungry, we go get what we want. Many of us probably cannot even imagine what it would be to be truly famished. I mentioned earlier the teenagers who participated in the 30 hour "famine" event to raise money for kids who don't have enough to eat. The event was a great concept. Not only did our teens help other children with the money they raised, but also, for those 30 hours they found out what it was like to have nothing to eat. It's good for us to recognize how blessed we really are.

Use food for the purpose for which it was intended. In the same light, feed your body foods it was intended to eat. A diet balanced with a mixture of fruits, vegetables, whole grains and lean meats allows your body to function in a healthy state. All foods should be consumed in moderation. Likewise, balance other areas of your life with regular exercise and plenty of sleep.

Jesus was tempted in the wilderness in three different ways, and one of them was with food, as we're told in Matthew 4:3, *"The tempter came to him and said, 'If you are the son of God, tell these stones to become bread.' Jesus answered, 'It is written: man does not live on bread alone, but on every word that comes from the mouth of God'"* (NIV). Jesus points out it isn't food He needs; it's His God who sustains Him. When we begin to let Jesus fill up the emptiness we've tried to satisfy with food, then we begin to find the satisfaction that food will never give to us. In John 6:54–58, Jesus said, *"Whoever eats my flesh and drinks my blood has eternal life, and I will raise him up at the last day. For my flesh is real food and my blood is real drink. Whoever eats my flesh and drinks my blood remains in me, and I in him. Just as the living Father sent me and I live because of the Father, so the one who feeds on me will live because of me. This is the bread that came down from heaven. Your forefathers ate manna and died, but he who feeds on this bread will live forever"* (NIV). The food the others lived on before they died never satisfied them, but Jesus says that in a relationship with Him, we will be satisfied.

There's one thing Jesus said in those scriptures that has always puzzled me. Why did he say "eat my flesh and drink my blood?" It sounds cannibalistic. Actually, Jesus was using a phrase a general might say to his soldiers before they went into battle in Jesus' culture. He was saying, "Fellows, as we go into battle, if you'll follow the orders I give you and give Me your complete, surrendered commitment, and if you'll eat of My flesh and drink of My blood, then we'll be successful." What he means is, "Commit everything to me, follow Me, and the victory is ours!" In other words, Jesus said, "Commit everything to me——even what you eat——and we'll be victorious, and I will fill your emptiness."

Maybe today you need to ask Jesus to forgive you for the sin of letting something else become your god——namely food. You can pray something like this, "Jesus, today I need Your help. I need You to fill up my emptiness on the inside. I ask You to forgive me for this dependency I have had on another idol, and make changes in me so I will let You be the One who cares for me."

Someone once wrote that he who fails to plan, plans to fail. Follow this advice when it comes to food. Plan ahead what you will eat and have available healthy choices in advance. Don't wait until you are hungry to find food. Because, if you do, you will be much more tempted to overindulge in the not-so-healthy food choices surrounding you. Thus the cycle of gluttony continues.

Be assured of this one thing; you can become free of gluttony or any other habit that is controlling you. Gluttony does not have to be a life-long struggle for you. When you commit to let Jesus control this area of your life, you can be free. He will not force Himself on you, but He will help you by the power of the Holy Spirit. Occasionally, He will heal a person instantly from a bad habit. But more often, His rescue comes through a steady walk toward deliverance. Seek Him for fulfillment and obey His direction.

ENVY

J ust after I moved to take a new senior pastoral position, in the community I lived a new church had recently started. It had around 50 members, and its pastor was a visionary with strong leadership skills. The people of that church seemed to love each other and had a desire to reach their community for Christ. I could have learned much from their model of ministry. But when their church outgrew mine, things began to change. Jealousy started to get hold of me, and I began to question why that kind of growth was not happening in my own church. This other church grew from 50 to 500 people. It got to the point that I couldn't even pass by the church. Every time I saw the pastor, I would experience feelings of envy and jealousy. In my mind, his success pointed to my failure, and I simply couldn't face it. It was eating me up on the inside. Just like Solomon said in Proverbs 14:30, "...*envy rots the bones*" (NIV).

Since that church was across town, I was relieved I didn't have to look at it on a regular basis. But it quickly outgrew the building it was in, and wouldn't you know it, the church moved into an old grocery store only three blocks from my church. I believe God was thinking it was about time He really straightened me out in the area of envy.

So they moved in and hung up their cool sign. They even had a golf cart taking people to the front door. We didn't have golf carts. They had everything going for them; their church was growing, and it was great. Jealousy worked up so much in me that I couldn't even enjoy the good things God was doing in my church, because I was so focused on what was happening over there.

One day my wife Kristi and I were driving past that church as we always did on our way home. My frustration had grown so that I would not so much as glance that way. Kristi is my conscience sometimes, and she asked, "What's wrong? You can't even look over there now?" That's when I realized how pathetic it was to be a grown man acting like a small child.

Identify

It's easy to say that envy is a childish thing. I believe people often think that only children get jealous, and it's for reasons such as: another kid has a toy that the other doesn't have, or one child is a teacher's pet and the other is not. Perhaps that's one of the reasons why it's so hard for us as adults to admit we have an issue with jealousy. It is child's play. We must realize how childish it really is to be envious of someone else to the point that it eats us up inside.

Jealousy causes us to do all sorts of strange things. We may criticize people's talents, their money, their jobs, their good lives, their marriages, their health and their looks. With envy we look at them and we feel badly about what they have that we don't. Then we pull ourselves away. We say things like, "Well, I just won't be around them and feel badly about myself when I'm there." While referring to the nice guy in the office we might say the guy is "just a little *too* nice." Or in reference to a beautiful woman, we might jealously say something like, "She is just *too* pretty. She's got the whole Barbie thing going on with the hair and the tan. Pretty is okay, but she's sickening. Let's get simple and conservative." Or, in regard to a family that is financially stable we could be heard reflecting, "If I had their money, I wouldn't spend it the way they do."

Jealousy creeps into our brains and begins to poison our thoughts and attitudes. We begin to think things such as, *My kids are smarter than their kids, so why are they getting all the breaks? My kids are just as good at sports; they ought to be starting. They must be buying the coach doughnuts or something.* Our thoughts become full of accusations like, *You know how she got that promotion? She's been taking the boss out to lunch.* Jealousy and envy lead us to believe that other people get more than they deserve, and we only get compensation. They could be the hardest workers or far more qualified than others for the position, but we become convinced they get better than what they deserve. And yet, we're convinced that the things we don't get are because of who we are. Envy is a deadly thing in our lives. But just how deadly can it be?

Envy means feeling better only when someone else is failing. For instance, a jealous person might say to someone, "Oh, your car? You were in an accident! I always liked that car." But he or she thinks smugly to himself or herself, *They shouldn't have had it anyway; well, they'll be driving an old clunker before long. Too bad.* Someone might say, "Oh, you lost your job. You loved that job, and that was a good-paying job too." But he or she may spitefully think, *He lost his job; good. Things won't go as well for him now.* These examples show the ugliness of this sin. They show what coveting does to us and how it distorts our views in relationships.

Envy exiles us from God's perfect plan. Each of the seven deadly sins will cause us to become isolated. But I'm using the word *exile* in this chapter because it illustrates what happened to the children of Israel after they coveted their neighbors' lifestyles.

The Israelites had a prophet named Samuel to guide them. They considered God to be their king, and Samuel spoke the words of God. He was God's voice. Yet, the Israelites began to look around at all the other nations and compare themselves. All of the other nations had kings. So they went to their prophet and said, "Samuel, we think you're doing a good job, but we want to be like everyone else."

In 1 Samuel 8:4-7, we read, "*So all the elders of Israel gathered together and came to Samuel at Ramah. They said to him '... now appoint a king to lead us, such as all the other nations have.' But when they said, 'Give us a king to lead us,' this displeased Samuel; so he prayed to the LORD. And the LORD told him: 'Listen to all that the people are saying to you; it is not you they have rejected, but they have rejected me as their king...'*" (NIV).

This is one of the most disheartening verses in the Old Testament, and it is a pivotal point in the history of Israel. God gave them what they asked for and things definitely changed for the people. I'm not sure how God shows emotion, but in that verse you can almost sense His tears. God was taking care of them, had provided for them, and helped them. But their envy had caused them to want someone else to lead. God even let the people know that a king would not be good for them because he would tax them, cause their sons to go to war and bring about bondage.

"... 'Now listen to them; but warn them solemnly and let them know what the king who will reign over them will do.' Samuel told all the words of the LORD to the people who were asking him for a king. He said, 'This is what the king who will reign over you will do: He will take your sons and make them serve with his chariots and horses, and they will run in front of his chariots. Some he will assign to be commanders of thousands and commanders of fifties, and others to plow his ground and reap his harvest, and still others to make weapons of war and equipment for his chariots. He will take your daughters to be perfumers and cooks and bakers. He will take the best of your fields and vineyards and olive groves and give them to his attendants. He will take a tenth of your grain and of your vintage and give it to his officials and attendants. Your menservants and maidservants and the best of your cattle and donkeys he will take for his own use. He will take a tenth of your flocks, and you

yourselves will become his slaves. When that day comes, you will cry out for relief from the king you have chosen, and the LORD will not answer you in that day.' But the people refused to listen to Samuel. 'No!' they said. 'We want a king over us. Then we will be like all the other nations, with a king to lead us and to go out before us and fight our battles.' When Samuel heard all that the people said, he repeated it before the LORD. The LORD answered, 'Listen to them and give them a king.'" (1 Samuel 8:9-22 NIV).

God warned them of the consequences of having a nation with a king, but told them that if a king was what they wanted, then they could have it. God does not force anyone to follow His plan. Instead, He invites mankind to join Him in it and allows each individual to choose whether to walk God's way or not. The Israelites chose the plan they saw the world around them using.

Saul became the first King of Israel. Throughout the book of 1 Samuel, we see that though he started as a good king, Saul's envy and arrogance drove him to ungodliness. Further in the Old Testament, we find that the tribes of Israel became very quarrelsome over their kings who ruled after Saul. Their nation lacked unity and was permanently divided because of this. Many of their future kings led the nation into idolatry and acts of abomination and disobedience before God. Eventually, because the people followed the rule of earthly kings, the nation of Israel, like the others around them, was taken into captivity. They were exiled, and this exile meant they were taken away from the people and land they knew and loved. All of this happened because they envied other nations and because they wanted what everyone else had. It eventually caused them to be separated from the valuable security God had provided them.

The Bible has several stories of how envy destroys. In the very first chapters of the Bible we see where Adam and Eve envied God's wisdom, so they ate of the fruit and were exiled from the garden (Genesis 3). And in Genesis 4, Cain looked at his brother Abel and was disappointed and envious because God favored Abel's offering more than his own. Cain's jealousy drove him so far as to kill Abel. After the murder, God approached Cain and declared his fate, *"When you cultivate the ground, it shall no longer yield its strength to you; you shall be a vagrant and a wanderer on the earth"* (Genesis 4:12 NASB). Cain's response shows his despair at the consequence of his envious additude and actions. Verse 14 reads, *"Cain said to the LORD, 'My punishment is too great to bear!'"* (NASB).

Like Cain, jealousy severs our relationships with God and others. When you and I envy, we react by pushing people away and isolating ourselves from them.

The Bible does very well at understanding human nature and talking about envy. James 3:16 says, *"For where envying and strife is, there is confusion and every evil work"* (KJV).

The scriptural word *envy* the author uses here is the same word used for a zealot. A zealot is someone who is fixated or obsessed with something. So envy could be an obsession with an individual who seems to have a better life. The person looks better, has more money, is more popular, has more influence, and on and on. And if the obsessive fixation on someone in an envying sort of way continues, the natural progression will be strife.

The word *strife* is the same word used to describe a political party. I'm sure you can see the connection there. A political party works by finding like-minded people, forming an agenda or a platform, and then working with diligence to make sure their platform progresses. They will do whatever it takes to make sure everyone knows what they believe. James is saying that when you and I get fixed or obsessed on somebody else, who in our minds has it so much better, we begin to seek other people who feel the same way about that person. We ask until we find them. We ignore the people who don't agree and keep inquiring until we find people who do. We find one person, then another, until all of a sudden there's this whole alliance gathered up just nitpicking at another individual. Because of the jealousy *we* have inside toward this person, we cannot see him or her in a correct view. Strife is taking place. So envy starts, then strife, and then it turns into confusion.

Confusion is a synonym for disorder or anarchy. Envy and strife continue until it begins to hurt. All rational thought is lost when envy and jealousy are in the mix. Usually, we demonize such a person when envy is in play. We see no good in the person and begin to believe he or she is all bad. We tend to read something into every word he or she says and every action he or she takes. The reaction to these assumptions is hostility.

If we don't stop envy, it will turn into strife, and then it will turn into confusion. But it doesn't stop there. The last thing James says is that it will be *evil.* The Greek word here for evil is *phaulos,* which literally translates as *foul* or *flawed,* and figuratively means *terribly bad* or *wicked.* So if envy develops at our workplaces, it will eventually become foul. If envy grows in the church, we will have a stinking mess on our hands. The progression James explained is that if envy is not quickly stopped, alliances are formed to work against the coveted person until the situation becomes a worthless mess. This is precisely what the deadly sin of envy can do to our circumstances.

In Matthew 20, Jesus describes the kingdom of God by telling a story about a guy who owned land that needed to have work done on it. The landowner went into town at nine o'clock in the morning, and he saw some guys hanging out. So he asked a few of them if they wanted to go to work for him for a good day's wage. They agreed, so he took them out to the farm to do the work that was needed. At noon the man went back into town and saw more people standing around so he took a few of them back to work on the farm too. Again at 3 o'clock, he invited the people mingling around to come to work, and they agreed. Finally he made one more trip into town at 5 o'clock and picked up a few others milling around; they returned with him to work for one hour. Some of these people had been working since 9 o'clock in the morning while others had just been there since 5 when the whistle blew for quitting time at 6 o'clock. All the workers lined up to receive their checks. The guys who showed up at 5 o'clock were handed a day's wage. So the workers who had been there all day expected a bonus, even though they had agreed previously on the pay for a day. When they received the same amount as the last shift workers they protested, "Wait a minute. That's not fair!"

The moral to this story is that the kingdom of God is truly a kingdom of grace. But Jesus also teaches us something here about jealousy. This story teaches us that envy and jealousy cause us to be unhappy with what we've been given. In Matthew 20:3 it says, *"At nine o'clock in the morning, he was passing through the market-place and saw some people standing around doing nothing. So he hired them"* (NLT). This sounded like a pretty good deal for these guys. They might not have received work and been able to feed their families, and then a guy came out of the blue and said, "I don't know you, and you don't even have to fill out an application. Come on, I'll give you a job for today." When they agreed to work it sounded like a pretty good deal. Well, let's see what their response was upon payment. In verses 10–12, it says, *"When those hired first came to get their pay, they assumed they would receive more. But they, too, were paid a day's wage. When they received their pay, they protested to the owner. 'Those people worked only one hour and yet you've paid them just as much as you paid us who worked all day in the scorching heat.'"* (NLT).

Envy has a way of cancelling out gratitude. For example, a few hours earlier the guy complaining didn't have a job or a paycheck. Then he was given a job and a day's wages, but he couldn't be happy with that because envy distracted him. His jealousy caused him to miss out on being thankful for what he had already been given. Has that ever happened to you? You're perfectly happy with your own house until you showed up on the doorstep of somebody who had a bigger house. Or maybe you loved your big-screen TV until you found a bigger one. That's what envy does to you. Envy will never be content with what it has; it will always want something bigger and better.

What else can we learn from this story about what jealousy does to us? The resentful workers were fortunate to even get a shot at work. They might have had to work all day, but at least they got a job. Now talk about getting a break, the latecomers only worked one hour, and they got a full day's pay. Obviously, they got a sweet deal that day and were blessed. But envy does not allow the begrudging to be happy for others.

Deliver

Love—not envy—allows us to be happy for others and thankful for what we have. In 1 Corinthians 13:4-6, Paul says, *"Love is patient and kind. Love is not jealous or boastful or proud or rude. It does not demand its own way. It is not irritable, and it keeps no record of being wronged. It does not rejoice about injustice but rejoices whenever the truth wins out"* (NLT). When somebody gets a break and is blessed, love stands up and says, "Good for you!" Whereas envy says, "That is not right."

Jesus taught if we're going to fulfill the commandments, we have to love God, and we have to love others. He said, "*By this all will know you are My disciples, if you have love for one another*" (John 13:35 NKJV). First Corinthians 13 makes it clear that with envy and jealousy in our lives, we cannot fulfill the command of loving others as Jesus has asked us to do. Coveting leads to anger and doesn't allow happiness.

Envy also causes us to resent the giver. Verse 11 of Matthew 20 says that the workers received their pay and then protested to the owner. Now consider this. If you're upset over the supposed injustice, you're ultimately upset with the one handing out the gifts. So in reality, when you have jealousy in your life, the issue is not really with the person you envy. The issue is with God. You might not say it. You might not verbalize it, but in essence you're thinking, *God, You ripped me off! You didn't give me a body like that person. You didn't give me a job like that person. You didn't give me the money or the house or the stuff. You have all the resources at Your disposal, but You chose to give to somebody else and not to me. My issue is with You.*

The time you find yourself taking issue with God, is the time to be delivered from jealousy and envy. However, to be delivered from them you will have to acknowledge the truth.

In Jesus' parable of the Kingdom of God, the landowner represents God Himself. Verse 15 quotes the landowner as responding to the question of wages, "*Don't I have the right to do what I want with my own money? Or are you envious because I am generous?"* (NIV). In essense he was saying, "I choose to give out grace to everybody." The landowner gave a job to at least one man when he didn't deserve it. He gave extra pay to another when he didn't deserve it. Why? Because it was his to do as he wanted, and what he wanted was to dispense grace.

Think about how this applies to us. If we're going to participate in building God's Kingdom, then we've got to understand the concept of grace. After all, we cannot ask God to help us if, at the same time, we are thinking God is the one ripping us off. In other words, we cannot trust God for help if we think He's the problem. The best thing we can do is to just be honest with God about the whole thing. We need to go before Him and say, "I'm coming to you honestly, God. I need help getting this envy and jealousy out of my life. As it is now I can't stand to look at this person. This is the way I honestly feel." Then take the next very important step and say, "Lord, forgive me."

To be delivered from envy and jealousy, you and I have to change the price tags. What you and I consider valuable must change. In fact, I'd like you to ponder this question: why would you consider people who have more money, different facial features, a different body, or a better job as better than you? Who defined what is good and not so good? Who said you have to look a certain way to be beautiful? Who said you must earn a big salary to be wealthy? I can tell you who didn't say these things: God. God never said if you have the big house, or the big screen, or the big promotion, or big beauty, "I'm pleased with you." God didn't have anything to do with placing price tags on things in our culture that seem so valuable to us.

God has said He doesn't look at things in the same way we do. In 1 Samuel 16:7 we're told, "...*Man looks at the outward appearance, but the Lord looks at the heart*" (NIV). Maybe we need to begin looking at things the way God does. Maybe we need to look at the real heart of the matter instead of continuing to be caught up in price tags and misplaced values.

What would you give to have wealth, beauty, popularity, or power? What would you sacrifice to obtain these or to own what someone else possesses? Measure yourself by your answers to those questions. The things for which you would give the most have the greatest value in your life.

How do we know what God values most? We know by observing what he paid the highest price for. God sacrificed His only Son Jesus in order to take away our sin, give us abundant life and share an eternal relationship with Him.

When you think about it, there's a lot of stuff we've put on a pedestal as valuable and important. We say to ourselves, "If I don't have this, I'm not happy. If I don't have that, I'm not all that I should be." But what's all this stuff got to do with anything eternal? We need to get to the point where we can say, "This stuff is nice, but it's not what life's all about." What's valuable is the ability to love, the ability to build relationships, and the ability to be content. Have you asked the Lord to forgive you for having the wrong value on things? Learning to value the godly gifts people have can help us deal with envy and jealousy. We must learn to admire without comparing.

I often enjoy listening to the financial advisor, Dave Ramsey. In my opinion, Dave is a great communicator. I've followed his principles on finances over the past 10 years and listened to him convey truth in simple, matter-of-fact ways. But since I'm also a public speaker, I'm confronted with a choice. I could be tempted to look at Dave Ramsey and think, *Well, doesn't he think he's something. He's up there making all that money. Sure he's got financial peace.* However, I've always enjoyed learning from people. So, instead of envying his popularity, I've chosen to listen to Dave so I can learn from him. His illustrations are great, as is the way he communicates, and I enjoy his humor. So instead of comparing myself to him, I can just learn to admire him and learn from him.

The band in my church inspires me. Often I admire how well they all play their instruments. In school I was a drummer, but let me tell you, I am not a good metronome. I can't even keep a beat. I enjoy our band's talent every Sunday. I can't sing or play, but what a blessing to know we're all blessed because they can.

Recognizing people's gifts is very beneficial. Perhaps you know somebody who knows how to make money. Well, praise the Lord for that, and may God help them to use the money to benefit others. It is not a sin, and it is not a bad thing. The point is, we are to be blessed with what God has given wherever He has given it.

To really be delivered from envy and jealousy, you must recognize how rich *you* really are. In Philippians 4:11–12 Paul said, *"I am not saying this because I am in need, for I have learned to be content whatever the circumstances. I know what it is to be in need, and I know what it is to have plenty. I have learned the secret of being content in any and every situation, whether well fed or hungry, whether living in plenty or in want"* (NIV). Paul has told us that he has learned the secret of being satisfied, and now he's ready to give us that secret in verse 13: *"I can do everything through Him who gives me strength"* (NIV). Paul has learned to be content because he knows God's got him covered.

God supplies everything we need. We are rich, and God will take care of you and me. Our greatest treasure is the fact that God loves us. He sent Jesus to express how much He loves us. *"God showed how much he loved us by sending his one and only Son into the world so that we might have eternal life through him. This is real love—not that we loved God, but that he loved us and sent his Son as a sacrifice to take away our sins"* (1 John 4:9-10 NLT). In reading that scripture we can hear God call to us, saying, "I sent My only Son, Jesus, to die for you because I love you. If you'd been the only person walking around this globe I'd still have sent Him for you to let you know I love you and to make a way that your sins can be forgiven so you can have a relationship with Me. You are My most valuable priority." In light of God's opinion of us, you and I are truly rich.

When we get past the point of looking at what we don't have, and instead begin looking at what we do have, then we will find ourselves stamping out jealousy in our lives. We're rich with grace and blessed beyond what we deserve. We showed up at 5 o'clock, and He has paid us a full day's wage. Out of His abundant love, He has shown us grace. So if envy is an issue in our lives, we must begin reflecting on what we have, and change the price tag on whatever is distracting us from *that* most valuable prize.

PRIDE

I believe that the number-one deadly sin is pride. Pride says, "They're so egotistical, but I'm self-confident. They're so vain, but I'm well dressed. They're arrogant, but I'm right. They're demanding, but I'm pursuing excellence. They're conceited, but I'm secure." In other words, we see one thing in others, but we see something altogether different in ourselves. We readily see flaws in others, but we struggle to see them in ourselves.

Furthermore, pride actually encompasses all of the other sins. Famous author C.S. Lewis said that gluttony, anger, greed, and drunkenness are mere flea bites in comparison to pride. After all, it is through pride that the devil became the devil. Pride leads to every other vice, and Lewis says that pride is the anti-God state-of-mind. So it's no wonder God wants pride out of our lives and cannot work through us unless it's gone.

God will go to extremes to help rid us of pride. I've found, through my own experiences, that He will sometimes let us suffer the consequences of other sins in our lives just to get rid of the pride. He'll let us go through the consequences of blowing our top, screaming at other people, and losing friends and credibility, all the while waiting for us to finally realize it's our pride that got us into the situation in the first place. He will allow us to suffer the consequences of lust and experience enormous trials in our marriage until we realize it was our pride and our selfishness that got us there.

God disdains pride in our lives. The author of Proverbs 16:17-19 wrote, *"The highway of the upright avoids evil; he who guards his way guards his life. Pride goes before destruction, a haughty spirit before a fall. Better to be lowly in spirit and among the oppressed than to share plunder with the proud"* (NIV). The fact of the matter is that pride will mess up our lives. Nevertheless, most people have a hard time looking in the mirror and admitting a pride problem.

Identify

Let me tell you a story that Jesus presented about pride. It is found in Luke 16:19-31, which says, *"There was a certain rich man who was splendidly clothed in purple and fine linen and who lived each day in luxury. At his gate lay a poor man named Lazarus who was covered with sores. As Lazarus lay there longing for scraps from the rich man's table, the dogs would come and lick his open sores..."* (verses 19-21 NLT).

Let's pause here a minute because I want you to see this comparison. Jesus says there was a rich man who built a walled fortress to keep everybody out. This rich man clothed himself in fine linen even though just outside his gate lay a poor man, named Lazarus, who needed clothes and bandages for his sores. Every day the rich man walked by the poor man and offered nothing.

"...Finally, the poor man died and was carried by the angels to be with Abraham. The rich man also died and was buried, and his soul went to the place of the dead. There, in torment, he saw Abraham in the far distance with Lazarus at his side..." (verses 22-23 NLT).

Jesus taught that while on this earth it may have appeared to others that the rich man was more prominent than the poor man. But, in eternity, that is not true. The prideful man went to hell, but the one who was poor went to heaven. Heaven for Lazarus was to sit next to Father Abraham. For the Jewish people, Abraham was the patriarch of their faith. What a privilege for a man who had nothing on this earth to be feasting with and leaning against Father Abraham in heaven, while the rich man was distantly being tormented in hell.

This story describes something of heaven and hell, but more to the point, Jesus is demonstrating what it looks like to be prideful and what damage comes from it. Let's keep reading the story to observe the consequences of pride for the rich man.

Verses 24-26 say, *"The rich man shouted, 'Father Abraham, have some pity! Send Lazarus over here to dip the tip of his finger in water and cool my tongue. I am in anguish in these flames.' But Abraham said to him, 'Son, remember that during your lifetime you had everything you wanted, and Lazarus had nothing. So now he is here being comforted, and you are in anguish. And besides, there is a great chasm separating us. No one can cross over to you from here, and no one can cross over to us from there'"* (NLT).

It says that this rich man's pride caused him to be tormented in hell. The rich man is hollering over to Abraham pleading for Abraham's help. Abraham says, "I wish I could, but there's a large chasm here so we can't get together." One of the damages that can come from being prideful is that we isolate ourselves. Figuratively, that's what this story illustrates.

Isolation, as a result of sin, is a recurring theme in this book. Every sin — gluttony, laziness, anger, envy, lust — every one of them will isolate you in some way or another from God and others. I hope you've learned that. Pride is no exception. Conceit will isolate you from God and important people in your life. It will cause you to criticize others. This is because arrogance says everybody else is second-rate in comparison to you, your knowledge and your possessions. Pride can have such a grip on you that you may push everyone else away. But even when it has messed up your life, when you are left lonely and frustrated and you have no one else to lean on, pride will tell you it's everybody else's fault. Vanity will blind you to the truth. Just look at what it did to the rich man.

I think the most astounding part of this whole story is what the rich man does while being tormented in hell. I want you to notice how he addresses Abraham the patriarch and Lazarus the poor man. First of all he looks at Abraham, not Lazarus. Then he says to Abraham, "Tell Lazarus to get some water and bring it to me to curb my suffering." If we continue to read the story from verse 27, we find that the rich man says, *"Please, Father Abraham, at least send him to my father's home. For I have five brothers, and I*

want to warn them so they don't end up in this place of torment"
(NLT). Here is the man in hell, facing all the torments of that
place, and yet his pride stops him from even addressing the poor
man, Lazarus. He addresses Abraham with the attitude of, "You
and I are a little more equal; this guy's beneath me. Since he's
beneath me, would you please tell him to be at my beck and call?
Let him come to cool me off and tell him to go warn my brothers." Even in hell, this man is not aware of his arrogance.

To top this off, in verse 29, Abraham says, *"Moses and the
prophets have warned them. Your brothers can read what they
wrote."* And the rich man replies, *"No, Father Abraham! But if
someone is sent to them from the dead, then they will repent of their
sins and turn to God"* (NLT). Here is a man so prideful, even
while in hell, that he argues with Abraham, the patriarch of the
faith and a representative of God. Pride stops us from being
submissive to God and fools us into thinking we've already got all
the answers. So, with that attitude, why do we need God? Even
through his torment, the rich man's conceit was so great that he
was willing to argue with the authority of God. Pride is a spiritu-
ally-deadly disease. This story illustrates to us the consequences of
our self-regard. By humility, we inherit heaven—life and comfort
where we lean on others and share. Whereas big-headedness is a
fast track to hell—life alone and needy where one must shout in
order to be heard.

Pride hinders our focus. It tunes out God's voice and turns
off those around us. It will have such a grip on us that we'll be
unwilling to see our faults until it will eventually distort our

ministries. I've been in church since I was 12 years old, and I think the church has lost a lot of precious ground for the Lord because we've looked down our noses at other people. The main problem is that while we're looking down our noses at folks, we can not look up to God, where our focus should be. We look down on others when we think like this: *That person doesn't dress like he should.* Or *that woman's life surely isn't all cleaned up, is it?* In other words, we're really elevating ourselves by thinking, *I'm a little bit better than you.* And each time we do, we lose a little more ground for the Lord.

Along that same line, I find it interesting as a pastor that many folks will say, "Pastor, way to go! I'm glad you're preaching on sin!" The perplexity is that we as Christians like to hear sin sermons, but we give very few public confessions. Most of us think sin and hell sermons are for everybody else. That's why Jesus had this to say in Matthew 7:1-2: *"Do not judge, or you too will be judged. For in the same way you judge others, you will be judged, and with the measure you use, it will be measured to you"* (NIV).

That scares me; it humbles me. Jesus plainly says, "Larry, the way you judge others is how I'll judge you. If you judge others by the way they dress, by their job, by their talents or lack thereof, that's how you will be judged."

Jesus talked more about pride and judgment in the setting of the church in Luke 18. Beginning with verse 9, it says, *"Then Jesus told this story to some who had great confidence in their own righteousness and scorned everyone else. Two men went to the Temple to pray. One was a Pharisee, and the other was a despised tax collector,"* (verses 9-10 NLT).

He takes us to this temple and explains that there were two men, one who seemed very righteous outwardly who was a religious leader and another who was a tax collector—which, in Jesus' day, meant that he was a sinner and a social reject.

Jesus says, *"The Pharisee stood by himself and prayed this prayer: 'I thank you, God, that I am not a sinner like everyone else. For I don't cheat, I don't sin, and I don't commit adultery. I'm certainly not like that tax collector! I fast twice a week, and I give you a tenth of my income,"* (verses 11-12 NLT).

Wow! What a prayer. When this Pharisee came before God Almighty he said, *"I've* achieved this. *I* don't sin; *I* don't do the things that other folks do. I perform more religious acts than others. Thank you, God, for *my* accomplishments." With this story Jesus taught that pride causes us to measure our self-worth on performance and outward appearances.

On one hand, there's not necessarily anything wrong with being proud of a good accomplishment. The problem—the pride—develops when we build our self-esteem on what we have achieved or successfully portrayed. What happens when all that stuff comes crumbling down? What happens if the secrets that are hidden in our hearts become revealed to others? What happens when a husband comes in and says to his wife that he wants a divorce? What happens if a family member ends up in jail? What happens if we've built our confidence on temporary earthly things?

Jesus teaches us that we shouldn't build our lives on our deeds and achievements, but rather on a relationship in Christ. We build our lives on the fact that God loves us, He cares for us and it is in Him that we find our self-worth. God wants us to get to a point where we're not so concerned about what other people think. Prideful people may often say, "I'm good with that. I don't really care what other people think." However there's actually a huge difference in motives. For the follower of Christ, the motive is that we won't let other people's opinions become the focus of our lives. God is the one we want to please, and as long as we're pleasing Him, we'll do pretty well in our relationships. But on the other, the prideful person says, "I'm not interested in pleasing any other people because they're second-rate. I'm better than them, and their opinions don't count." The Pharisee, for example, looks at the tax collector and says, "Hey, I'm better than he."

Pride is always about competition. Its central thoughts are, *As long as I'm better than you, then I'm okay. As long as I've got more money than you and drive a nicer car, then I'm okay. As long as I have a bigger house, wear better clothes and people like me more, then I'm winning and you're not.* Then and only then is pride happy. The prideful man, Jesus says, looks at others and says, "At least I'm better than he or she is." It can be frustrating when we feel others don't take notice of us or when others get attention and we don't. Our pride finds itself in competition with others.

In Luke 18:13, we pick up the story again with Jesus saying, *"But the tax collector stood at a distance and dared not even lift his eyes to heaven as he prayed. Instead he beat his chest in sorrow, saying, 'O God, be merciful to me, for I am a sinner,'"* (NLT).

The real problem with vanity is that it wants you to think there's nothing wrong with you. Just like in the story, the tax collector could admit that he had a problem. But the prideful man dared not admit he had done anything wrong. Egotism always refuses to admit there's anything wrong. In verse 14, Jesus sums it all up: *"I tell you, this sinner, not the Pharisee, returned home justified before God. For those who exalt themselves will be humbled, and those who humble themselves will be exalted,"* (NLT).

Deliver

So, according to Jesus, what is the cure for pride? Humility. Humility is not something that we show, but it is essential if we're going to make it in life. I once heard that, "Humility is like underwear; it is essential but indecent if it shows." The main reason we should be humble is because Jesus was humble, and He's the ultimate example of God on this earth. What I really love about Jesus, among many things, is that He has great self-esteem. He is very comfortable with Himself, yet still humble.

We often think that if we can't be prideful, we must be one of those people who lets others walk on us. Yet, Jesus didn't let people walk on Him; He was in full control the entire time. He had strong self-esteem, but was amazingly humble. In Philippians 2:5–8, Paul says, *"Your attitude should be the same as that of Christ Jesus: who, being in very nature God, did not consider equality with God something to be grasped, but made himself nothing, taking the very nature of a servant, being made in human likeness. And being found in appearance as a man, he humbled himself and became obedient to death — even death on a cross,"* (NIV). When finding humility, our attitude should be the same as that of Christ Jesus.

Humility frees us from the "image factor." When you and I decide that humility is important, we're not worried so much about image as we are about Christ. We find freedom from that pressure. The prideful have something to prove, so they work to accomplish it through whatever means possible. But when you and I grasp this concept of humility, all of a sudden we don't have so much to prove because we ultimately desire to walk in the image of Christ.

There are three things we must do to develop humility. The first is to confess. With every sin that we've looked at, the deliverance has to start with acknowledgement. When we say, "Lord, I admit I am prideful," then we begin to experience humility. In Psalm 32:5, the psalmist said, *"'Then I acknowledged my sin to you and did not cover up my iniquity'. I said, 'I will confess my transgressions to the Lord — and you forgave the guilt of my sin,'"* (NIV). When I confessed, then I found forgiveness. One of the most profound steps we can take today is to admit that pride is a problem in our lives. We admit to ourselves, "I've got an issue here. I think I'm better than others. I'm not open to what God wants in my life because I think I've got it figured out." The first step to humility is to admit that we're prideful.

The second step to becoming humble is to learn to worship. When we worship, we're ultimately thinking about God, and He becomes our focus. In authentic worship, things are no longer about us. We acquire an attitude of humility. We do not dewll on thoughts such as, *They're not singing songs I like. I don't appreciate that arrangement. The pastor's sermon gets longer and longer week after week.* No! Worship is all about God—giving Him praise and honor because He's so worthy. Keep in mind that we need to practice worship not just on a Sunday but every day of our lives. As we spend time worshipping God, our attitudes will find humility, the cure for our arrogance.

Have you ever noticed that when you idolize something, you become like that something? When I was a kid, I had an idol, and his name was Elvis Presley. In fact, my mom made me an Elvis suit—a white jump suit. It looked good! I'd put that suit on and quiver my lip and shake my leg, and I'd do my best to sing "Hound Dog" because that was my favorite song. I wanted to be like Elvis, and so I tried very hard to imitate him. That's what you do when you idolize someone.

The same principle applies when we worship God. When you and I worship, it is a form of idolizing something, too. In Psalm 115:8 the psalmist said, talking about false idols, *"Those who make them will be like them, and so will all who trust in them,"* (NIV). As worshipers of Christ we idolize Jesus, the more we dote on Him, the more we become like Him. When we magnify Him every day of the week, our focus automatically shifts from selfish thoughts to God thoughts. When we pause in our daily routines to say, "God, I just want to take a moment to adore you," then the focus is off of us and on to God. And before you know it, we begin to be more like Jesus because humility comes through reverant worship.

Finally, we can attain humility through service. As the story goes, a man had the privilege of going to heaven and to hell. In hell was a huge banquet room with a large table and lots of food. Around that table sitting at a distance so they could not reach the food with their hands were the people of hell. Their chairs were too far back. They hollered at each other, they screamed at each other, their bodies were emaciated because they couldn't eat, so they were just overwhelmed with agony. The man said it was a tormented place. He saw the feast and the food, and it looked so good, but when he saw the people he thought what an awful place. Ironically, every person in hell who sat at the table was given a spoon. The spoon had a long handle on it, so they could reach the food with the handle, but as they tried to eat with it, the food always fell to the floor. It would add to their anger and add to their torment, and they would just sit day after day.

The man then went to heaven, where, ironically, he was confronted by a very similar scene. He walked into heaven, and there was a huge banquet room complete with a large table and a feast of food, and the people were still sitting at a distance from the table. They could not reach the food with their hands. Only this time the people were different. They were laughing, they were joyous, and they looked well-fed. Their joy overwhelmed the man as he watched. Everything seemed to be wonderful. He noticed, however, that just as in hell, each person around the table in heaven had a spoon with a handle long enough to reach the food, yet too long to eat with. The difference between heaven and hell was that those in heaven used the spoon to feed everyone else around them on the table. This story illustrates the joy in service, and the frustration in selfishness. When we serve, we not only become more like Jesus, but we also don't think so much about ourselves. The truth is, humility is not thinking less of yourself, it's thinking about yourself less.

If you want to develop humility in your life, I encourage you to serve. When we live to become servants of God and we step off the throne of our lives to serve others, we leave space for Jesus to make His home on the throne. Do an act of service this week but don't take credit for it and see how it changes you. It will help you to develop humility. In fact, make it a habit. Every day this week look for opportunities to perform acts of service and see the difference it makes in your own selfish pride.

Pride is a hard one to admit, and it's our greatest stumbling block. But blessed are we who recognize this sin and release to God His rightful throne in our lives. Permitting God Almighty to consume our thoughts and attitudes enables us to honor Him and serve in the kingdom of heaven—both now and in eternity.

CONCLUSION

As you have read this book, I hope you've grown tired of what sin is doing in your life. Through each chapter, I've tried to reiterate this very important point: Satan has a plan for your life. His goal is to kill, to steal and to destroy you. Satan wants nothing good for you. He doesn't want your marriage to work, and he doesn't want you to enjoy your friendships. He wants you to be frustrated with your life. He wants you to be depressed, discouraged and isolated. That's only a brief list of his derisive desires for you.

Jesus wants just the opposite. He said, *"I am come that they might have life, and that they might have it more abundantly"* (John 10:10 KJV). He freely gave Himself to accept the punishment for *our* misdeeds so we could be forgiven and live abundantly. We were spiritually dead in our sins, but He has given us a way out.

Through the simple act of believing, you can be born into a life that promises abundance. That doesn't necessarily mean material prosperity, but it does mean spiritual newness. Your spirit is made alive when you share a relationship with the God who created you—body, soul and spirit. He offers you His spirit and His abundance as you walk with Him.

"But the fruit of the Spirit is love, joy, peace, patience, kindness, goodness, faithfulness, gentleness and self-control..." (Galatians 5:22-23 NIV).

In other words, with the influence of His Holy Spirit, you have the power to live above anger, sloth, greed, lust, gluttony, envy, pride and any other sin that exists. You are empowered to be humble, respectful, grateful, loving and self-controlled. With provision such as this, why would you look anywhere else? Why would you live any other way?

My prayer is that through the last seven chapters, the Holy Spirit has helped you identify the sins that are destroying your life and relationships. Please be open to confess these to God and seek His deliverance. Be willing to submit to His authority and direction in your life. Take action steps to change, and lean wholly into Jesus who has come that you may have life in abundance.

ABOUT THE AUTHOR

Larry Morris has been a pastor for over 20 years and has a passion to help others understand Biblical truths in a practical sense. He holds a B.A. in Theology from Southern Nazarene University. He and his wife, Kristi, live in Oklahoma with their two children, Hope and Jason.

RESOURCES:

Jeff Cook, Seven (Zondervan, 2008)

Dan Boone, Seven Deadly Sins; The Uncomfortable Truth (Beacon Hill Press, 2008)

Graham Tomlin, The Seven Deadly Sins and How To Overcome Them (Lion Hudson plc, 2007)

Rick Renner, Sparkling Gems (Teach All Nations, 2003)

LaVergne, TN USA
23 August 2010
194274LV00002B/4/P